To B.J.:

Salud!

PUERTO VALLARTA
ON 49 BRAIN CELLS A DAY

Gil Gevins

COATIMUNDI PRESS
Oakland, California

Cover photos by Lucy Muniz.
Original cover concept by Lucy Muniz.
Cover design by Paul McBroome.
Design and layout by Paul McBroome.
Published by Coatimundi Press.

For Lucy

Contents

How I Fired My Boss

It was shortly after my arrival in Mexico that I decided to hold a surprise birthday party for my new bride. A surprise party is a foolish idea under the best of circumstances; in this case it proved to be nearly a fatal one.

We were enjoying a late lunch on Los Muertos beach when the misguided notion first wormed its way into my sun-addled brain. Just behind us a mariachi band was lurching its way through an off-key, ear-numbing version of "Guadalajara". Most of the restaurant's patrons, faded expatriate retirees who hadn't missed a happy hour in ten years, didn't seem to mind the music. Running a good four margaritas off the pace, I was not so fortunate.

Menu in hand, I motioned for the waiter and attempted to tell him in my most authoritative butchered Spanish that I was ready to order. Unfortunately, I committed a small error in pronunciation which changed just slightly the meaning of the phrase. Instead of saying, "Waiter, I am ready to order," I said, "Waiter, I am ready to urinate."

My wife turned beet-red with embarrassment and the waiter politely pointed out the general direction of the bathroom.

"Bathroom?" I said indignantly. "I don't want the bathroom. I want to urinate. Right here. At the table."

The waiter looked confused and a little sad. My wife kicked me viciously under the table—twice.

This was not the first time I had embarrassed my wife, who had lived in Puerto Vallarta for many years and spoke excellent Spanish, by my insistence on practicing my new language at every opportunity. The week before, at a party hosted by an important government official, I had verbally stumbled with even greater abandon.

The gracious host had taken me aside and inquired how I liked Puerto Vallarta.

"I love Puerto Vallarta," I replied sincerely.

"And what do you like most about Vallarta?" my host asked.

"The sun, the people, and the..."

At this point I had intended to say how much I loved the seafood (mariscos). But I became confused and substituted unwittingly the word "maricones," a sadly uncomplimentary term for gay men.

"I love the gay men!" I told my startled host. "They are delicious. The best I ever tasted. And so inexpensive!" I concluded, beaming with enthusiasm.

My host nodded somberly, turned and walked away.

A little later at the same party I capped off the evening by asking the nine-year old girl whose birthday it was: "So tell me, how many anuses do you have?" The poor thing turned bright red and fled for her life.

Back at the restaurant, my wife had finally tired of chewing me out and was munching on a plate of shrimp al mojo de ajo, when a covey of waiters suddenly surrounded a nearby table and, having first set a cupcake sporting a single candle before a couple of bone-white newly-weds from Nebraska, launched into the worst rendition of "Hebby Burrday" I had ever heard.

Birthdays, I thought to myself, everyone seems to be having a birthday. And Lucy's is coming up in two weeks. I know, I'll give her a surprise party to make up for humiliating her in front of half the town.

Back in those long-gone days, Puerto Vallarta was not the modern tourist destination it is today. It was a rustic little town where things were not so easy to arrange. Telephones were few and far between. Not many locals spoke English. And something simple like getting a drain unplugged could take days or even weeks. Realizing none of this, I foolishly set out to create a surprise party of truly Byzantine proportions.

In retrospect, my most serious blunder, aside from the decision to have the party in the first place, involved the fireworks. For some inexplicable reason, I *had* to have fireworks.

After a great deal of effort, I managed to acquire the approximate location of the quasi-clandestine fireworks factory. I set off in the early afternoon, behind the wheel of my Safari (a tin can like vehicle whose production was suspended in 1973 due to safety considerations).

The factory was supposed to be located on the outskirts of a small village called Coapinole an hour outside of Vallarta. The road leading to Coapinole was poor to non-existent, but I managed to find the place without too much difficulty.

Pulling up alongside a small general store I asked the proprietor, "Donde estan los cueteros?" *Cueteros* are the men who fabricate and set off fireworks. The man gave me a set of directions, the key component of which seemed to be a left turn at "el rancho".

I spent the next thirty minutes driving around in dusty circles in a vain attempt to find this rancho. I wasn't exactly certain what a rancho was supposed to look like, but I had in mind an image of the "Ponderosa" from the old Bonanza TV show: corrals, horses, cattle and pastures.

Needless to say, neither Hoss nor Little Joe was around to help me and I was reduced to repeatedly stopping and asking for fresh directions. But no matter whose directions I followed, I kept returning to the same two-story building where a wild party seemed to be in progress. From within its unpainted cinder block walls, earsplitting music, boisterous shouting, wild laughter and even the occasional scream could be heard.

Finally, I climbed out of the Safari and asked a staggering passer-by where the rancho was. He pointed drunkenly to the two-story building and said "Rrrrrrrancho!"

When I expressed my lack of comprehension, the man suddenly began to dance around in the dirt, gyrating his hips and making unusual grunting sounds.

My first thought was that he was doing an Elvis impersonation. But then it suddenly dawned on me: a *rancho* was, among other things, a whorehouse.

I turned left and drove to the end of the road where I found a barbed wire fence and a crude gate.

The trail was clearly marked and easy to follow. Down one hill. Up another. Through a small grove of coapinole trees. Past a herd of cows, etc.

After walking for about two kilometers, I cleared a small rise and came upon a sign set in the dirt which read: "Peligro" (danger). Ah, I must be getting close, I thought. A hundred meters further on was a larger sign bearing the same warning, and a hundred meters beyond that still another even larger sign with giant blood-red letters:

"PELIGRO!"

The fireworks factory, when it finally came into view, consisted of a thatched lean-to, several crude wooden benches and a long equally crude wooden table.

Three of the dirtiest men I had even seen were huddled together around the table connecting fuses to an enormous infernal-looking contraption I could not even begin to identify.

The oldest of the three came forward and greeted me effusively. He was short, stout and bore an enormous round scar on his shirtless torso. His hair, his skin and most of his clothes were covered with a thin film of black powder which, I later learned, was TNT. Thankfully, no one was smoking.

The old maestro and I got on famously, and I soon found myself in possession of three dozen rockets and a wheel-like device called a "corona". The maestro and his two sons gave me all manner of instructions and admonitions as to the proper handling of the fireworks, but they spoke far too rapidly for my inexperienced ear. In fact, aside from the price, all I was able to decipher with certainty was the word "peligroso" (dangerous), which they must have repeated at least ten times.

Back in town, I cached the rockets with a nervous neighbor. Then I went home and attempted to explain away yet another mysterious absence to my wife.

Lucy, not a jealous woman by nature, was beginning to suspect that I was having an affair. And I could hardly blame her. I had been taking an awful lot of long walks and aimless drives lately. Of course, what I had really been doing was inviting all of the guests, most of whom had no telephones.

This is, I discovered, the principle reason why having a surprise party for a spouse is such a stupid idea: lies, half-truths, devious behavior: no way to treat the person nearest and dearest to one's heart.

I had a feeling that Lucy was about to ask, "Who is she?" so I told her I was going down to the beach for a swim. Actually, I was on my way to a secret rendezvous with the off-key mariachi band.

By the time the fateful night had arrived, I had degenerated into the proverbial nervous wreck. A slight but persistent twitch had developed under my left eye and my lips had become bleached a whitish pink by over-doses of Maalox Plus.

But everything was arranged. At precisely seven-thirty the mariachis would come gushing into the house horns ablaze, followed by our twenty guests and the neighbors bearing the twenty T-bone steaks I had stored in their fridge.

The diversion—every surprise party must have a diversion—was a birthday dinner at the Camino Real hotel. Lucy had just finished dressing and was not in the best of moods. Aside from being largely convinced that I had been plowing in forbidden fields, she had never been in favor of the birthday dinner. What she really wanted, she had made clear on six or seven occasions, was (God help me!) a birthday party.

I withdrew the bottle of birthday champagne from the ice bucket (champagne at the Camino Real was out of the question) and popped the cork. This, of course, was the "signal".

In marched the mariachis playing "Las Mañanitas," followed by the throng of invitees. Lucy, taken miraculously, completely by surprise, burst into tears.

Words cannot express how elated I felt to see those tears of joy and the look of absolute love on my wife's blushing face. But I had no time to linger over sweet sentiments. So I gave my ecstatic wife one long passionate kiss, and then set to work, blithely ignorant of the fact that I was about to come frighteningly close to killing myself and many of my guests not once, not twice, but three separate times.

Several of the invitees had been assigned the various tasks of setting up the bar and schlepping the booze and such over from the neighbor's house. While they performed these critical functions I applied myself to the barbecue.

My impromptu grill (a rack purloined from our stove and supported by a bunch of bricks) held only five steaks, so I was beginning with a serious handicap. Hurriedly, I laid out a bed of charcoal on the ground in our small courtyard, only to realize that I had no starter fluid. This was a serious problem. In those days, self-starting briquettes, or briquettes of any kind were not available in Puerto Vallarta. Charcoal, of the homemade variety, was purchased at lumberyards.

I panicked for a moment before remembering that I had a half a liter of Raicilla (Mexican moonshine) stashed under the kitchen sink next to the Drano. Raicilla, I had once been told, has such a high alcohol content that it could be used as a charcoal starter.

As I stood dowsing the coals with Raicilla, my boss walked over and asked if I needed any help.

"Maybe, Fernando," I said. "I'm trying to light the charcoal with Raicilla. We might have a lot of huffing and puffing to do."

Fernando sipped his vodka and laughed good-naturedly.

"Lighting a barbecue with Raicilla; that's the funniest thing I ever heard."

"Well, it's either that or eat our meat raw," I said, taking out a match. "So, here goes nothing."

I tossed the match onto the coals, not expecting much in the way of a reaction.

"Hiroshima, but on a smaller scale," was how it was later described.

Fernando and I instinctively jumped back, but not before we had lost various hairs on many of the exposed portions of our physiognomies. My boss, luckily for me, was not a shorts man. The thermal blast had badly singed his lower trousers, which, much to my dismay, were actually smoldering.

"Jesus, I'm sorry, Fernando," I exclaimed. "I had no idea."

"No problem," Fernando said shakily. "I think I spilled my drink."

As Fernando stumbled off to get a refill, Bobby, a hypochondriac time-share salesman who also happened to be a Vietnam vet, walked over and said, "Jesus Christ! If we'd had that stuff in Nam we could've won the war."

In any case, the Raicilla turned out to be an amazing charcoal starter; it didn't just start the coals, it immolated them. Within minutes they had all turned a lovely uniform white.

Everything was moving along beautifully now. My wife was in heaven. The guests were eating, drinking, dancing and laughing their hearts out. The steaks were popping off the grill like clockwork, cooked to perfection. I only had one small problem. There were twenty-two guests and only twenty T-bones. I had no choice but to eliminate two meat eaters.

"Bobby," I said, "you want to hear the dumbest thing?"

"Was it something I said?" Bobby asked defensively. Besides being a hypochondriac, Bobby was also a certified paranoid schizophrenic.

"No, this kid who works at the butcher shop," I said. "This kid tells me, as I'm walking out with twenty T-bones, that there's some kind of new microbe they've discovered that doesn't affect the cows but is fatal to humans. I said, 'kid, you better get another job.' Can you believe..."

Bobby had already begun to back away from the barbecue pit, covering his nose and mouth with a handkerchief.

My next victim was Roger, another time-share salesman who was a fairly serious alcoholic as well as the most shameless freeloader I had ever met. Roger was always the first to arrive at a party and the last to leave, as long as the booze held out.

I did not have to seek Roger out. He was operating on a tight schedule which brought him by the barbecue area every five minutes to see if his steak was ready.

"Roger, I told you, we're serving the ladies first."

"No problema, no problema," Roger said, taking a huge gulp from his giant glass of vodka. "Did I mention, rare is fine? I'm not fussy. I can eat it practically raw."

I knew exactly what Roger was up to. He was hoping to double-dip: get one rare T-bone early, then an over-cooked one late.

"Roger," I said, dropping my voice to a confidential whisper. "I've got a problem."

"What's that?" Roger asked, inching closer.

"We're going to run out of booze, especially the vodka. Could you help me out? Run down to the corner and pick up a couple of bottles of Smirnoff's?"

"Sure, sure, no problema," Roger replied.

"Thing is, I'm out of cash," I confessed. "I'll pay you back later."

"No problema."

Roger turned and headed straight for the bar to top off his half-full glass. That took care of steak number two. Roger would be passed out in half an hour at the most. We'd just plant him off in a corner of the garden where he'd be out of harm's way.

By eleven o'clock, the food was gone, the booze was, in fact, running low and the mariachis had packed up and gone home. Roger had been dragged under an avocado tree where he was snoring contentedly. All that remained to cap off a wildly successful night were the pyrotechnics.

While my wife and most of the guests gathered in our small canyon-like courtyard, I climbed up to the third floor of the house and out onto a narrow cement ledge. It was from this precarious perch that I planned to manually launch the three dozen TNT-loaded rockets.

I picked up the first projectile and examined it uncertainly. The truth is, I had never set one off before and was not sure how to proceed. I was looking at a fat, five-inch long cardboard tube with a long stick attached to it. The fuse was located at the bottom of the tube and seemed awfully short for such a long rocket.

Should I hold the rocket by the tube (three of which would have made a nice stick of dynamite) or by the long flimsy stick?

Holding onto the tube as I lit the fuse did not seem like such a swell idea. What if, instead of launching itself skyward, it simply exploded? Somehow, holding it by the long flimsy stick didn't feel entirely right either. But in the end, I opted for the stick.

Holding a cigarette in my right hand and the stick in my left, I shouted, "Here goes!" to the crowd gathered below.

Just as the tip of the cigarette was about to make contact with the fuse, however, someone screamed: "NO! NO! STOP!"

It was Ubaldo, the only person at the party who had ever lit a Mexican rocket before.

"Not the stick!" Ubaldo yelled. "You hold the rocket! Not the stick!"

Suddenly, in a flash of lucidity, I realized that the stick was located below the rocket, thus placing it, as well as my hand, squarely in the path of the rocket's fiery thrust.

So I grasped the fat cardboard tube gingerly in my left hand (if the launch goes awry, I reasoned, at least I'll still be able to write my name), touched the cigarette to the fuse and held my breath.

The rocket ignited and I fought the strong urge to

immediately let it go. You have to allow the rocket to gather a bit of momentum, I had been told, before you release it. While I waited the second or two for this momentum to build, I tried my best not to pee in my pants.

But up it soared high into the sky in a beautifully straight trajectory, before exploding with a huge, thunderous bang.

Down below, everyone clapped and cheered. I took a theatrical bow, and nearly fell off the narrow ledge.

By the tenth rocket, I had gained a certain degree of confidence. By the twentieth, I was beginning to feel a little cocky, which was not wise.

On the twenty-first launch, I decided to release the rocket with a stylish flick of the wrist. Unfortunately, the flick threw off my timing and the rocket took a nose-dive straight into the garden.

"Run!" I screamed. "Inside! Everybody inside!"

As the rocket attempted to burrow itself into the ground, most of the guests ran screaming into the house. My boss, Fernando, and Roger were two of the exceptions. Fernando, his reflexes slowed by one double too many, made it to his feet and had taken only two unsteady steps before the rocket exploded. Roger, passed out on the ground not ten feet from the blazing tube, was of course in no condition to go anywhere.

The blast, focused by the four walls of the small courtyard, was unbelievably loud. Fernando, already dazed and confused by the alcohol and his near death experience at the barbecue pit, belatedly covered his ears and began to stumble around in circles, mumbling, "I'm deaf. I'm deaf. I'm deaf."

Roger's reaction was somewhat less orthodox. Like a man who has been awakened from a dream in which he is being chased by a shark, Roger, lying prone on his belly, began to wildly thrash his arms and legs in a fruitless attempt to swim across the courtyard.

I raced down the stairs and up to my boss. "Fernando, are you all right?" I demanded.

"What?" he said, shaking his head like a wet dog.

"Are you okay?" I repeated.

"What?"

Fernando's hearing loss was only temporary but I did not know that at the time. I began to review in my mind the availability of alternative career choices.

"What about the corona?" Ubaldo asked.

Ah yes, the corona.

The corona is a wheel-like device made of bamboo sticks with *four* rockets attached to it. It is set upon a pointed stake and lit. In theory, it begins to spin around and around until it has acquired sufficient thrust to lift itself up into the air, where it spirals high into the sky emitting copious showers of sparks and smoke.

I decided to set off the corona out in the street where there was more room. The street, Basilio Badillo, was a heavily trafficked road even in those days, but it seemed a better choice than the courtyard.

"How do we anchor the stake?" I asked Ubaldo.

"I don't know," Ubaldo shrugged. "With some bricks or something."

I placed a stack of bricks all around the stake, set the corona on top and put the end of a lit cigarette to the fuse.

The fuse, which contains several firecrackers just to make things more interesting, exploded—which was normal. The corona began to spin around, which was also normal. Then the stake, which I later learned should have been buried at least a foot deep in the ground, fell over.

The corona, prematurely separated from its launching pad, began to hop and skip insanely around the street before finally coming to rest under the gas tank of a parked car. As the smoke continued to billow and the sparks to fly out from under the car, everyone scattered.

"It's gonna blow!" Bobby, seized by an involuntary Vietnam flashback, screamed.

The entire street filled with smoke as traffic came to a standstill and everyone waited, from a safe distance, for the impending explosion.

Interestingly enough, the gas tank did not explode. But by the time the smoke had cleared out, so, too, had all of our guests. Except for Roger, who (having failed to breaststroke his way out from under the avocado tree) had slipped back into sweet dreams of open bars, complimentary buffets and generous, willing women with large breasts and no limits on their credit cards.

The Fridge
Over The River Quale

"Hormones," my uncle announced authoritatively, "are responsible for more than eighty per cent of man's behavior."

That assertion, implying as it did the ability to quantify human nature, was the type of facile nonsense which, under ordinary circumstances, I would have dismissed with a laugh. But my uncle, in addition to being one of the most respected endocrinologists in the world, was a man at whom one only thumbed one's nose from a safe distance.

"I'm sorry," I said carefully. "I'm not sure I understand what you mean."

"You watch the Discovery Channel." My uncle, it was clear from his tone, was making an accusation, and not asking a question.

"Well, I suppose…" I began defensively.

"Then you have, I imagine, seen groups of male baboons performing acts of ritualized aggressive behavior in an apparent attempt to impress the fertile females?"

"Of course," I said. "Who hasn't?"

"That behavior," my uncle explained, "is the precise hormonally inspired equivalent of what takes place every night in Carlos O'Brien's. Especially in low-season."

"So according to you," I said, becoming upset, despite myself, "human beings are little better than animals."

"Not at all," my uncle replied with infuriating calm.

"Humans are simply passing through a relatively early stage of their evolution."

"Well, I'm sorry," I told my uncle, "I just don't see what the big deal is. Everyone knows that sex and hormones go together."

"Have you ever come across a female quail hunter?" my uncle demanded slyly.

"What?"

"A woman who derives pleasure from trudging through the woods shooting small defenseless birds with a powerful firearm: have you ever known one?"

"No," I said warily, "I can't say that I have."

"What about a man who becomes excited almost to the point of sexual arousal at the mere prospect of purchasing a new refrigerator?"

My uncle had, once again, painted me neatly into a corner with his superior and inspired logic. If there was one single thing in all the world which I personally despised, it was shopping for large expensive kitchen appliances. For my wife, on the other hand, buying a new stove or refrigerator was an act of pleasure so intense it made the multiple-orgasm pale by comparison.

We had already been to three-quarters of the major appliance stores in Puerto Vallarta. Now, as yet another unctuous little salesperson stepped smartly forward to greet us, my small reservoir of patience, shallow to be begin with, had all but dried up.

"Welcome," this individual announced cheerfully. "My name is Pablo. How may I be of service to you?"

I had a ready reply to this question, but I prudently kept my mouth closed.

"How much is this refrigerator?" my wife asked, indicating a model we had more or less agreed upon several stores ago.

Pablo proudly named a figure, which sounded suspiciously familiar.

"Satisfied?" I said. "It's the same price everywhere. Let's just get it."

"Alright," Lucy said, her face flushed with excitement. "As long as I can have the Darth Vader door."

"But that's five-hundred pesos extra," I moaned. "What's wrong with the yellow door?"

"I want the Darth Vader door," Lucy insisted sweetly but firmly.

The door in question was a strange reflective black color and did indeed look remarkably like Darth Vader's face shield. Well, what the hell, I thought, desperate to get the whole business behind me.

Turning to our smarmy sales representative, I said, "Look, Pablo, we're going to buy this refrigerator with the Darth Vader door (*con la puerta estilo Darth Vader*). But it's the same price in every store in town. So why should I buy it here?"

"We give a one-year guaranty," he replied with a totally straight face.

"So does everyone else," I said.

"We also arrange personally for delivery?" he offered uncertainly.

"Unbelievable," I exclaimed. "By the way, Pablo, how much *is* the delivery charge?"

"Oh, very little," Pablo said vaguely.

"How little?"

"I'm not sure exactly. That's handled by another company—specialists in refrigerator deliveries," he added nervously.

"I'll tell you what, Pablo. You pay for the delivery and I'll buy it right now."

"No, no, I'm sorry. We cannot do that. We never do that. Nobody does that."

I grabbed Lucy's arm and began to steer her towards the door.

"Okay, Señor. Okay. Okay!"

The fridge was supposed to arrive at our house at four o'clock the following afternoon. By five, Lucy was bursting with impatience.

"Maybe the truck had an accident," she said.

"Honey, the store's only ten blocks away," I said reassuringly. "They're just late."

At six o'clock we attempted to call the store, but there was no answer.

"Something's wrong," Lucy said, "we better go down there and find out what's going on."

When a short while later we pulled up in front of the store, we found a small crowd gathered around an old battered truck with its hood in the *up* position. A very young man, who appeared to be the driver, was holding a rusty voltage regulator in one grimy hand and a bag of potato chips in the other. In the back of the open pick-up was a tall carton the approximate size and shape of our refrigerator.

I recognized Pablo, our sales representative, standing in the crowd pulling anxiously on a cigarette.

"So, Pablo," I asked him, "what's happened to our refrigerator?"

"Oh, I'm *so* glad you're here," he said, gushing with the enthusiasm of an undertaker at a longevity convention. "As you can see your refrigerator has been successfully loaded. But there's a small mechanical problem with the delivery vehicle. Please come this way."

Pablo led me over to the adolescent who was holding the voltage regulator, and formally introduced us. Meanwhile, six or seven other men were standing around with their heads under the hood, talking animatedly and gesticulating wildly at this or that automotive widget.

"Is that your Volkswagen?" the child-driver asked me after first stuffing his mouth with a fresh fist full of potato chips.

"Yes, it is," I replied, wondering idly which of the two varieties of grease he was ingesting (automotive and vegetable) contained the most cholesterol.

"Could I borrow your voltage regulator for a minute?" he asked, spraying my chest with tiny bits of yellow mush.

"I don't think so," I said.

After several minutes of fruitless discussion I offered to drive our refrigerator delivery specialist to an auto parts store.

By the time we returned the crowd had grown considerably and now included three policemen.

The new voltage regulator was quickly installed, but to no effect.

It was then spontaneously decided to jump-start the truck by pushing it down the street. There being no shortage of enthusiastic volunteers, the maneuver was soon underway.

While Lucy and I watched anxiously from the sidelines, eight men, including the three policemen, got the truck up to speed, as our refrigerator bobbed and weaved in the back like a small boat floundering on a choppy sea.

We watched the truck creep around the corner and disappear in the general direction of the River Cuale, still being manually propelled by the platoon of volunteers. I turned to my wife, who was looking a little pale.

"Want a Valium, honey?" I asked her.

Lucy indicated to me in so many words that this was not the moment for levity.

What seemed an eternity later, the truck appeared coming around the corner and glided silently to a halt in front of the store, exactly where it had started. Many of the volunteers, who had pushed the truck for approximately half a kilometer, looked as if they were about to drop dead.

"It wouldn't start," the child-driver informed me unnecessarily.

I leaned inside the cab of the truck to ask him what he intended to do next and noticed that the ignition key was in the *off* position.

"Didn't you turn on the key?" I asked incredulously.

"What for?" he replied. "That's why we were pushing the truck."

"Have you ever attempted to jump-start a motor vehicle before?" I asked.

"Well, um, no, not exactly," he replied defensively.

At this point, with my wife on the verge of hysteria, darkness falling and a sharp pain beginning to form behind my left eye-ball, I decided to take matters into my own hands.

The driver was reassigned to the rear of the truck where he was instructed to hold on to our refrigerator for dear life. Then I climbed grimly behind the wheel, roused the troops, turned the key to the *on* position and off we went.

The slow bumpy ride around the block proved to be surprisingly pleasant, if uneventful. I particularly enjoyed being pushed across the bridge over the River Quale, which at that time of the year was full of turgid cheerfully rushing water.

Steering the still moribund vehicle back to the curb, I hopped out just as it began to rain. Several of the volunteers dropped panting to their knees while their friends laughed and poked fun at their pathetic lack of manly stamina. Off in the distance, thunder could be heard. It began to rain harder.

More helpful curiosity seekers materialized out of the increasingly wet air and, impervious to the rain, began to argue over the true nature of the truck's mechanical shortcomings. Not a few of these new arrivals seemed to think for some reason that it was all the policemen's fault.

Lucy, meanwhile, had flagged down a passing pick-up and slipped the driver fifty pesos. With very little urging, a throng of good Samaritans made quick work of the transfer, and thirty minutes later the ordeal was finally over.

Sitting in the kitchen, a towel wrapped around her head, her face aglow with pleasure, my wife stared lovingly at her new acquisition.

"Aren't you happy we got the Darth Vader model?" she asked.

"Hormones," I muttered to myself. "He must be right; it's the goddamn hormones."

"What?"

"Yes, honey," I said, downing my shot of Raicilla in a single gulp, "I'm so happy, I feel just like Obi Wan Kanobee."

The Day Of The Iguana

Over the years a number of incautious gringos have, while under the influence of Raicilla, committed some truly memorable acts of stupidity. Scanning down the list of my own contributions to this colorful tradition of expatriate *tontorias*, I believe I can point with a certain perverse pride to what has come to be known as *The Day of the Iguana*.

The whole pathetic episode began on one of those perfect, pristine winter mornings at Las Animas Beach, in those long ago idyllic days before the advent of the booze-cruise, the beach vendor and the jet-ski. My new bride and I (we had been married for only three months) were sitting side-by-side in a pair of canvas chairs, holding hands and wallowing in the utter serenity of the wonderfully deserted beach. Overhead, a chorus line of graceful palms, swaying with the light morning breeze, left us bathing in a deliciously dappled blend of sun and shade. At our backs, the lush Sierra Madres climbed theatrically up towards the sky while, facing us, the friendly surf lapped affectionately at our toes.

The only manifestation of man's presence on the entire unsullied beach was a lone, haphazardly built palapa restaurant, which provided us, simply but effectively, with all of our corporal needs: oysters, fish, shrimp and liquids of varying toxicities.

Of all the recreational beverages available to us, the mildest and most mundane was beer, while the most fierce and exotic was Raicilla.

Raicilla, a rare form of mescal, and the only variety to possess true psychotropic properties, is distilled from the maguey cactus in the remote hills south of Puerto Vallarta. John Houston, an early gringo connoisseur of the beverage, is alleged to have described it as "a bewitching blend of LSD and unleaded gasoline". Bill Reed, Houston's biographer and drinking companion, once informed a reporter from the Los Angeles Times that Raicilla was "stronger than brake-fluid, but somewhat less corrosive than battery acid". From personal experience I had found Raicilla to make an excellent charcoal starter, as well as an effective disinfectant.

Happy as a turtle nosing his way across a scum-filled pond, I raised my gaze to the skies, tossed down my third Raicilla of the morning and shouted, "Praise Allah!" at a passing school of sardines.

Lucy, my supernaturally tolerant wife, cast a curious glance my way and said, "Better take it easy; you're a long way from Mecca, honey."

"No, I'm serious," I said.

"You're serious?" Lucy asked, her eyes wide with alarm.

"Yes. Look at those *fish!*"

Not fifty yards from where we sat the ocean was literally aboil with massive numbers of highly agitated sardines, all of whom were desperately fleeing for their little lives.

"Look, they're all just eating each other!" I shouted. "Can you believe it? One minute, you're a sardine, swimming along nonchalantly…"

"Nonchalantly?"

"And the next minute, you've been eaten by a bonita. Then a roosterfish eats the bonita. And then a dolphin eats the roosterfish. Then the…"

"So what's the point?" Lucy asked.

"The point? Well…for one thing, it's a perfect metaphor for unrestrained capitalism. Not to mention, life in general.

Survival of the…"

"I think it's time for your nap, honey."

By the time I had washed down my second plate of raw oysters with my fifth shot of Raicilla, it had been decided by the unseen forces which had temporarily taken control of my mind that Lucy and I were going to move to Las Animas on a permanent basis the following Monday. Then, as the world around me began to dissolve, along with significant portions of my forebrain, I became completely lost in a strange, absorbing reverie:

There was, it seemed, a serious difference of opinion between myself and a non-existent landscape architect (an arrogant fellow whose face had been disfigured by an enormous banana shaped scar, but who still bore a strong resemblance to Bill Dana), over the proposed location of the multi-tiered artificial waterfall and gazebo complex, which would shortly form the centerpiece of our Las Animas estate. The dispute between myself and the over-bearing landscaper quickly turned personal, and a number of serious insults were exchanged. The next thing I knew, machetes had been drawn and we were about to slash each other to ribbons when I felt a gentle tap on my shoulder. Twisting violently around in my beach-chair, I came nose-to-nose with a humongous iguana.

"Hello," I said politely.

The beast gave me a long baleful stare. Then it spoke to me, but in a language I did not understand.

Christ, I thought to myself, a talking Iguana!

Lunging from my beach chair in a mad uncoordinated rush to reach my feet, I tripped all over myself and landed flat on my face.

Lying there facedown on the warm sand felt, in my transcendent state, rather pleasant. In fact, I could easily have spent the rest of the day there had I not suddenly remembered the talking iguana. Scrambling to my feet I soon relocated the iguana who, it turned out, was being held expertly in the arms of a small barefoot boy.

"Quieres comprarla?" he said to me.

"Christ!" I screamed at Lucy, "Check out this iguana!"

"It's beautiful," Lucy said.

"Quieres comprarla?" the little boy said again.

"What's this midget trying to tell me?"

"He's not a midget," Lucy replied calmly. "He's a little boy. And he wants you to buy the iguana."

"Buy an iguana?" I said. "Buy an iguana? What a concept!"

Lucy naturally had no inclination to buy a six-foot long reptile, but she did seem to enjoy its company. So I bought everyone a drink, and the four of us sat ourselves down in the shade for a while, the very picture of familial harmony.

Most normal people, after consuming six shots of Raicilla before noon, begin to notice (if they are still conscious) an unusual preternatural glow pervading their surroundings. Colors appear, to their alkaloidally enhanced vision, amazingly vibrant, and even the most mundane objects (beer bottles, wooden chairs) seem to breathe with a Divine inner life of their own. In such an altered state of awareness, where even a crumpled napkin can become imbued with cosmic significance, the iguana was totally boggling whatever was left of my mind.

(Scientists have estimated that you pay for each shot of Raicilla with the loss of approximately forty-nine brain cells.)

For quite some time I sat contemplating this stupendous creature, with its jewel-like display of green, gold, black and orange scales, its icy warrior's gaze, its pure primordial perfection. I was transfixed—no, I was beyond transfixed; I was riding the crest of some life-altering epiphanic wave. Finally, after what felt like an eternity, I turned to my wife and said, "Honey, I'm in love."

"I love you, too," she said.

"I mean, with the iguana," I said indiscreetly.

"Gee, thanks," Lucy said.

"No, you don't understand. The thing is…I love you both. But of course I love you more," I added quickly.

Lucy gave me a long, hard appraising look.

"We'll call him *Ziggy*," I announced, as suddenly I was overcome with a feeling of paternal joy so intense it made my ears burn.

"No. No. No," Lucy said calmly but firmly, as if she were disciplining a puppy.

Even as my mind skidded hither and yon in those nether regions of indeterminate reality, I knew better than to argue the point openly with my wife. And so, while she was visiting the ladies room, I slipped the little boy five dollars. Then we shook hands to cement the deal and he passed me the short length of twine which he had wrapped around the thorax of my newly adopted son.

When Lucy returned a few minutes later and took in the fact that I was holding Ziggy in my arms, and that the boy had vanished (to go buy himself three cases of Coke), a short but lively discussion ensued. My wife was of the opinion that I had come temporarily unglued, and should refrain from making any potentially significant decisions until "later".

"Later," I said, "has such a vague ring to it. How much later?"

"Much, much, much later," Lucy said.

"Alright," I agreed. "We'll take Ziggy home, and then much, much later we'll decide whether or not to keep him."

Las Animas Beach was, and still is, accessible only by boat. We had been dropped off there that morning by a panga (motorized canoe), and now a little after five, the same boat returned to collect us. When the driver, an amazingly short man with the typical Australoid features of a Kiwi Islander, realized that he had acquired a third passenger, his nut-brown face took on a highly pained expression. Turning to Lucy, he said something to her in Spanish, which to my ear sounded a bit harsh.

"What'd he say?" I asked.

"He told me that you're throwing your money away on all that Raicilla," Lucy replied, "because you could achieve the same effect by simply sticking your head in a blender."

"There goes his tip," I said.

"He also said, 'tell your loco esposo to sit in the front of the panga, as far away from me as possible'."

"No problema," I said, giving the driver my friendliest smile. He did not smile back. Instead he glanced briefly about the boat, searching, I suspected, for a harpoon.

Fortunately for all concerned, it is a characteristic of iguanas that when they are held tightly, and feel that they have no possibility of escape, they usually go completely limp. Thus was I able, without incident, to clutch Ziggy closely to my chest, with his chin resting tenderly upon my shoulder, for the entire ten-minute ride back to Boca De Tomatlan.

The moment we climbed from the panga and began to wade across the chilly Tomatlan River, we were approached by a *beach-boy* named Miguel. Miguel was twenty-five years old and disgustingly handsome. Some people, especially North American women approaching retirement age, found him to be highly charming, as well. And I could see why. With the scruples of a perfectly tanned python, the sincerity of a Speedo-clad scorpion, and the compassion of a well-muscled Moray eel, Miguel was indeed a perfect paradigm of his breed.

As a matter of fact, most beach-boys fit Miguel's general description, though some were better at what they did than others. The precise nature of what they did for a living tended to vary along with one's point of view. In their own eyes, they were highly specialized tour-guides who catered to foreign women of a certain age. Offering a full range of services, their most arduous duties entailed falling in love (as often as twice a week) with the client of the moment. They were also required to be wined, dined, fussed over and made to receive lavish presents. In short, when the phrase, "the only sharks in Puerto Vallarta are on the beach" was coined, it was mainly the beach-boys the minter had in mind.

"Hey guys! How you doin? Long time no-see!" Miguel called out to us in his obnoxious beach-boy English.

"Miguel," I said without enthusiasm, "you're a long way from your feeding lanes today."

"What?"

"Long time no-see," I said.

"Hey, nice iguana!" Miguel exclaimed. "What you goin to do, eat it?"

Lucy and I smiled politely and continued to walk up towards our car.

When we failed to laugh at his joke, Miguel felt compelled to laugh for us. "Ha! Ha! Ha!" he said, falling in beside us.

If there exists in all the world a laugh more obnoxious or less sincere than that of the beach-boy, I have never heard it.

"Hey," Miguel said, as if the thought had just occurred to him, "you guys got a car here, or you goin to swim home?"

With the greatest reluctance, I admitted that we did indeed have a vehicle nearby.

"Wow! Great! Fantastic!" Miguel enthused. "How about givin me a ride to Vallarta? I got to meet my fiancée and I'm late already."

"You haven't met your fiancée, yet?" I asked innocently.

"What?"

"Sure, you can have a ride," Lucy said, smiling faintly.

"Wow! Great! Fantastic!"

Lucy opened the door of our VW bug and Miguel climbed into the back. "Wow, thas a big iguana, man," he said. "I don think it fit in this little car."

Lucy climbed behind the wheel while I maneuvered Ziggy and myself into the front passenger seat and closed the door. Due to his B-movie size it was necessary to wedge the iguana's head under the glove compartment, crowd most of his torso more or less into my lap and distribute his gargantuan tail throughout the backseat area.

"Miguel," I called over my shoulder, "do me a favor, please?"

"Sure, anythin, man. Whatever you say. What you need?"

"Hold on to his tail," I said. "We don't want him smashing up the car."

Miguel grasped the tail in both hands and laughed with macho bravado. "Ha! Ha! You guys are crazy; you know that? Ha! Ha!"

The first five minutes of the forty-five minute ride home passed uneventfully. Lucy drove, watching Ziggy uncertainly out of the corner of her eye. I sat in my seat, feeling drunkenly pleased with myself. With one hand I held down what would have been the iguana's neck, if he had had one; with the other I held down his hindquarters.

"Beautiful day," Miguel announced, simply because he was incapable of keeping his mouth shut for more than two minutes at a time. "Sun, beach, water. What else you need, right? I love nature. I'm completely a natural person."

At that precise moment, as if taking umbrage at the beach-boy's last dubious remark, Ziggy began to manifest the first signs of a disturbing incomformity with his present circumstances.

"Good Ziggy," I cooed soothingly. "Everything is okay. You're okay. I'm okay. Even Miguel is okay."

"What's the matter?" Lucy asked archly, "your son getting restless?"

"A little," I replied, clamping down a bit harder on the wriggling reptile.

"Hey man," Miguel cried out suddenly. "Stop de car. Stop de fuckin car!"

I glanced back over my shoulder and noted with concern that Miguel was no longer in my field of vision, and that Ziggy's tail was wagging with unfettered fury all over the backseat area, producing loud "THWACKS" every time it connected with the rear window.

Returning my full attention once again to the monster in my lap, I exerted even greater downward pressure with my right hand in a desperate attempt to keep Ziggy's head tucked safely under the dashboard. Meanwhile, bizarre muffled cries, interspersed with ear-splitting "THWACKS", were bubbling up to my ears from somewhere behind me. I soon realized that Miguel, scrunched down on the floor between the seats, was attempting to communicate with me in his native tongue.

"What's he saying back there? I asked my wife.

"You don't want to know," Lucy replied. "Though I can tell you this: it has something to do with your mother."

"THWACK! THWACK!"

"Stop de car, you crazy cabron!" Miguel screamed, colorfully combining his languages. "Ouch! Caray! Ouch! Stop de fuckin car! Hijo de la chingada!"

"Are you calling my wife a cabron?" I asked Miguel. "I'm sure you realize that she's the one who's driving."

"Grrrummmph. Mummph. Owwwww!"

"Better step on it, honey," I told Lucy. "I can't hold this thing much longer."

Lucy, who is an excellent driver, put on some more speed, as we continued to zip along the curvy coast road.

It was taking all of my rapidly waning strength to hold Ziggy down now. His killer-tail continued to rake the backseat like a fat bullwhip. The beach-boy's muffled shouts and screams (his head, I assumed, must have been wedged completely under the seat by now) had given way to muffled whining and moaning.

"Hang in there, Miguel," I shouted over my shoulder. "Another half an hour and you're home free."

"In half hour, I goin to be dead, you sick sonvabitch," Miguel replied in a muffled sob.

"You know something, honey? " I told my wife.

"What?"

"Ziggy is about to get loose. I think it's time we began to consider Plan B."

"And what would that be?"

"THWACK! THWACK!"

"Well," I said, "I imagine Plan B would involve stopping the car, for starters."

Like Mario Andretti pulling in for a pit stop, Lucy steered unhesitatingly off the road, skidding to a halt in a cloud of dust on a small rise overlooking the ocean.

"Now, I think we should open the door," I went on.

Lucy obediently opened *her* door.

"THWACK! THWACK!"

"No, no, I mean *my* door!" I screamed. Ziggy had finally managed to free his head, and his clawed front feet were about to gain a dangerous toehold in the vicinity of my crotch. "We need to open *my* door!"

"Be my guest," Lucy said unhelpfully.

"My hands are kind of full right now, honey," I gasped.

"Oh?" Lucy said, examining her nails.

"Honey," I said desperately, "he's starting to dig a hole—in my lap!"

"Your lap?"

"THWACK! THWACK!"

"Yes, he's…arrrgh!"

I'd never seen my wife move so fast. Before you could say "counter-tenor" she had leapt from the vehicle, raced around to my side and flung open the passenger door.

Ziggy and I tumbled out of the car more or less at the same time. But before I could scramble out of harm's way, he nailed me a good one on my leg with his tail. Then he was gone, scooting down the embankment and into the ocean.

Lucy and I stood holding hands and watching our ex-stepson swim off into the sunset.

"Look at that little sucker go," I said proudly. "He must be doing four knots."

The liberated reptile was indeed swimming effortlessly, using his powerful tail to propel him in a straight line directly towards Las Animas.

"Isn't this romantic?" Lucy sighed.

"Yes," I agreed.

"How's your crotch?"

"Fine."

"And your leg?"

"A little tender," I admitted.

"So, everything's okay," Lucy said.

"Yes," I said, summing things up, "all's well that ends well."

"All's well? All's *well*?"

It was a battered and disheveled beach-boy who, after untangling himself from the depths of the backseat, was now standing, frothing at the mouth, directly behind us.

"Oh, Miguel," I said pleasantly, "are you all right?"

"No, I'm not all right," the angry beach-boy snarled. "I'm very not all right. You goin to pay for dis. I'm goin to sue you for everythins you worth!"

"Sue me?" I said, laughing. "Miguel, we're in Mexico."

"So what?"

"So, I don't think you have a case."

"Oh, I have the case," Miguel fumed. "I have the case, alright."

Then it occurred to me, perhaps Miguel was right. In Mexico, though often unenforced, there are laws against almost everything. I turned to my wife. "What do you think, honey—would 'cruelty to beach-boys' constitute a felony, or just a simple misdemeanor?"

What The Hell's A Tejon?

"What in God's name is that?" Paul bellowed.

Paul was a tad tight.

"Looks like a baby anteater," I shouted back. My face was only inches from that of my friend, but I was if anything a tad tighter than he.

"There are no baby anteaters in Puerto Vallarta," my wife giggled.

"Of course they have anteaters in Puerto Vallarta," Paul snarled. "This is the tropics."

"Well, actually," I said, "this is the sub-tropics."

"Tropics, sub-tropics, neo-tropics, post-neo-sub-tropics. What the hell's the difference!" Paul growled.

Meanwhile, the furry brown creature with the four-inch body, five-inch tail and two-inch nose had begun to chirp with alarm. It was tied by the most meager length of twine to an old car battery someone had dumped on the beach a few feet from our table.

"Paul, you're scaring the poor thing," Lucy chided.

"Paul, you're even scaring me," I admitted.

"That's all right, I scare myself all the time. Muchuchu!" Paul boomed in his butchered Spanish. "Vengo aqui!"

A small, barefoot shirtless boy who seemed to be the creature's caretaker edged warily over to our table.

"Que esta el animalo?" Paul thundered.

The boy winced and said it was a baby "tejon", which did not tell us much. "Que es un tejon?" Lucy asked.

Grateful to be addressed finally by a human being, the boy told us that a "tejon" was a "tejon".

"What?" Paul cried.

Lucy translated. "He said that a tejon is a tejon."

"Well. That's the most mind-bogglingly stupid thing I've heard all day," Paul snarled in disgust. "And that includes everything I've said myself."

"I think we should take it home and upgrade its lifestyle," I said.

"Upgrade its lifestyle?" Paul said savagely. "What are you, out of your mind?"

Sanity is, of course, a relative concept. Sitting in direct, October sunlight and consuming over a liter of raicilla between us in the reality-blurring splendor of Las Animas beach had probably not been the most prudent way in which to spend a peaceful Sunday morning. But insane?

Yes, I suppose one could say that by this time we were all relatively insane—which explains, at least in part, what was to follow.

Two hours later we were back at our house in downtown Puerto Vallarta. We were seven dollars and four hundred and ninety brain cells poorer but we had, as the saying goes, gained a tejon.

A luxurious ten-foot length of string now tied this adorable little mammal to the avocado tree in our courtyard.

"What now?" Paul rumbled. Like a car without gasoline, Paul, without a steady stream of raicilla trickling down his throat, was beginning to sputter to a halt.

"It's probably hungry," Lucy said. "We better feed it something."

"Right. Paul, see if you can round up some ants."

"How do I do that?"

"I don't know. Scoop some up or something."

"Scoop some up?"

"Yeah, well…"

"*Scoop* some up?" Paul ran his fingers through his big bushy head of white hair and scratched his equally hoary white chin. "Twenty years in the CIA," he grumbled, "I've been asked to do almost anything you can think of. Poison African dictators. Seduce the daughters of Presidents. Crawl on my belly through…"

"Paul…"

"Live on nothing but worms and bird droppings in the jungles of Formosa."

"Paul, you're a civilian now," I reminded him.

"Thank God for that," Paul declared in his deep melodious baritone. "At least now I can sleep at night."

'You don't do such a bad job of sleeping in the daytime either," I said.

"Oh, you're not going to start on that 'when are you going to get a job' business are you?"

Paul had been living with us, on the cuff, for over a month while he got his "head together".

Lucy, with far more experience in the field of Puerto Vallarta insect life than Paul and I put together, disappeared into the kitchen. Several minutes later she emerged grasping between her thumb and forefinger by the tip of its antenna a slightly smashed cockroach the size of a Polaris submarine.

Ever so gently she laid it on the ground near the baby tejon.

"I may be stupid," Paul said, scratching his belly, "but isn't that a cockroach? I know cockroaches and ants both have six legs a piece, but…"

"Just wait," Lucy said serenely.

In a matter of minutes the mangled roach was covered by a small sea of ravenous ants.

The wee tejon sniffed at this feast-in-progress, but showed no inclination to partake himself. This untoward development threw us all into a state of befuddled consternation.

"Hmmm," I said.

"This reminds me of that time in Borneo…" Paul began.

At that precise moment something quite extraordinary occurred. A very small bird suddenly fell out of the avocado tree and landed at the little tejon's feet. The bird appeared to be perfectly healthy and there was no logical reason why it should have fallen out of a tree. Be that as it may, its apparent state of good health lasted less than one second. With truly demonic speed, our little furry friend broke the bird's neck and began to feed. In a matter of seconds, all that was left of the bird was a small mound of feathers and a detached beak.

Paul, Lucy and I stared at each other in open-mouthed astonishment.

Paul, with his CIA training, was naturally the first to recover. "That definitely ain't no goddamn anteater," he declared.

"No kidding."

"You better get out the dictionary," Lucy said.

Five minutes later I returned to the courtyard.

"Bad news," I said. "According to the *Larousse* (which is never wrong), a tejon is a badger."

Paul broke into a fit of violent laughter.

"Why is that bad news?" Lucy asked.

"Your husband bought a baby badger," Paul said with malicious glee. "A badger! Pound for pound the most vicious mammal on the face of the earth!"

"So a badger doesn't make a good pet?" Lucy asked anxiously.

"A badger does not make a pet at all," I said sadly.

"I can't believe you paid seven dollars for a badger," Paul cackled.

"You know, I'm not so sure," I said. "I've seen pictures of badgers and I don't remember them having such long noses."

The next morning I went out to the courtyard to find Lucy feeding TJ (our baby monster's new name) a handful of raw shrimp and scratching it behind its round, furry ears.

"It's so cute," Lucy sighed.

"Yeah. Like a Filipino on a Saturday night," I said, quoting a favorite line from Raymond Chandler.

My wife, no fan of the mystery novel, regarded me strangely.

A short while later our friend Nacho came by the house.

Nacho, a blond-haired Mexican of Russian extraction, had a mind like an encyclopedia, filled with all manner of mostly useless information. Nacho took one look at TJ and said matter-of-factly in his perfect, slow motion English, "Oh, I see you have acquired a baby coati."

"Wrong, Nacho!" Paul, already well into his first pint of raicilla, bellowed authoritatively. "It's a badger."

"I am afraid I have to differ with you, Paul," Nacho replied. "It is true that in Mexico this animal is referred to as a tejon, which literally does mean badger. However, 'tejon' is a misnomer. It is actually a 'coati'. Far from being a badger, it is rather in the raccoon family."

"You mean, it's like a tropical raccoon?" I said hopefully. "I've heard of people having raccoons as pets."

"Is it a male or female?" Nacho inquired.

"Hah!" Paul said. "You think Jungle Jim here knows if it's a male or female? Yesterday, he thought it was an anteater, for Christ's sake."

Nacho gingerly lifted TJ's long ringed tail. "It's a male," he announced. "That is unfortunate."

"Why?"

"The females live in groups with their young, are quite gregarious and relatively tame. The males, on the other hand, live by themselves, are called 'Solitarios' and are notoriously less tame. In fact, given that it is a male, I advise you to dispose of it as soon as possible—definitely before its fangs grow in."

But it was far too late to "dispose" of TJ. Lucy had already fallen in love with the little monster. And, if the truth be told, so had I.

Finding food for TJ proved to be no problem whatsoever. He ate everything: eggs, chocolate, meat, fruit, chicken, granola, seafood—in fact, like most of the children I knew, he ate everything except ants, vegetables and cockroaches.

We purchased TJ a red cat collar and a long thin metal chain which we attached to the avocado tree. By the time he was two months old he had grown considerably larger and had managed to defoliate the entire area. He had also, on several occasions, slipped out of his collar and explored the kitchen, "removing" everything from the shelves in an astonishingly short amount of time.

"That is the most destructive animal I have ever seen," Paul snarled.

"He is not destructive," Lucy said loyally. "He's just hyper-active."

Proudly doting father that I was, I preferred not to be judgemental. To me TJ was simply someone who liked to keep busy digging, climbing, doing somersaults, juggling empty plastic Clorox bottles and chewing on our extremities.

By the time he was six months old, our son was more or less full-grown, weighing in at fifteen pounds. His nose was longer than ever and unbelievably flexible. In fact, TJ's nose seemed to have a life of its own, moving this way and that in a never-ending search for esoteric scents.

"The coati has the most highly developed sense of smell of any mammal," Nacho had informed us one evening over dinner. "It can smell danger from over a mile away. Another unusual characteristic of the coati," Nacho went relentlessly on (by now even the waiter was beginning to nod off), "is its reversible rear ankles. It is able to rotate them a full one hundred and eighty degrees, thus enabling it to run straight down a tree as well as straight up. In addition..."

"La cuenta!" Paul screamed.

At ten months TJ achieved sexual maturity. We knew this to be the case because he had suddenly begun to stalk our cat (an orange tabby whose name was also Nacho) with a most lascivious look in his beady brown eyes. Nacho the cat happened to be of the masculine gender, but TJ, desperate to get his paws on anything small, four-legged and furry, did not appear to notice.

Finally, one day TJ nabbed the cat and began to make suggestive thrusting motions with his pelvis. We were a bit shocked at first, but the cat didn't seem to mind so we decided to allow nature to take its meandering course.

"Gay inter-species sex!" Paul grunted with disgust. "After two tours in Nam I thought I'd seen everything."

On what we estimated to be TJ's first birthday we threw him a small party. There was no cake, but after a raw surf and turf dinner TJ was treated to a small saucer of Piña Colada. TJ loved his cocktail and the alcohol did wonders for his normally aggressive personality. For the very first time he became calm, affectionate and cuddly. He even stuck his tongue in my ear.

By the time TJ was approaching his second birthday he had begun to act strangely. His collar seemed to be annoying him and he spent hours on end reaching behind his head with his forepaws trying to unbuckle it.

One day he finally succeeded. Thus liberated, he immediately scooted over the seven-foot high wall, beat up the neighbor's pit bull, headed for the hills and was never seen again.

Years later, I still think about TJ. I imagine him scampering around the jungle, and I hope that all of that time he spent practicing on Nacho the cat paid off for him in the end.

Total Immersion

I had been living in Puerto Vallarta for almost three months and was, like many new arrivals, feeling somewhat frustrated by my inability to connect with the local culture. Part of the problem was my lack of language skills. Unable to communicate with the many marvelous Mexicans I met, most of my new friends were turning out to be Americans and Canadians whose greatest concern was how many English language channels they could receive with the illegal black boxes attached to their satellite dishes. My wife, to whom I expressed this frustration on a daily basis, counseled me to be patient, that opportunity would soon knock.

And knock it did, in the form of an invitation to attend a wedding in the tiny pueblo of Las Gardenias, some two and a half hours north of Vallarta. "It's kind of rustic out there," Lucy warned me. "Are you sure you want to go?"

"Are you kidding?" I cried gleefully. "This is what I've been waiting for: a chance to totally immerse myself in Mexican culture!"

Las Gardenias was little more than a long dirt road dotted with shacks. But despite its simplicity it possessed, for me at least, a great deal of charm. Chickens, pigs, dogs and burros wandered the village freely, while an abundance of banana and palm trees gave the place a lush, tropical air. As we pulled up to the tiny adobe-walled church, I felt as if we had entered an enchanted dream, as if we had gone back in time to a more pure, more innocent era.

The interior of the church was heartbreakingly humble: dirt floor, a patched-together roof, unadorned walls and no pews. But it was packed to bursting with chattering people, bouquets of colorful flowers and a quintet of confused doves, who had flown in through a hole in the roof and couldn't find their way out again.

Since the poor church contained no furniture of its own, everyone had brought wooden folding chairs from their homes. By the time we arrived all of these chairs were occupied, including several pairs which had been placed before the altar. Standing between these last chairs were Paco and Eva, the bride and groom, so small they looked like children. And facing them was the Padre, who had just cleared his throat and was about to begin the ceremony.

Our arrival, for some reason, brought everything to a grinding halt. Paco and Eva seemed surprised, even alarmed, by our presence. After consulting briefly with the Padre, Paco approached my wife and they held a short conversation in Spanish.

"He wants us to be padrinos," she said, turning to me. When I shrugged with incomprehension, she added, "A padrino's a godfather."

"You mean, like Marlon Brando?"

A vision flashed briefly before my eyes of a long line of Mexican bakers waiting to kiss my ring, and then asking me to have their neighbors' legs broken.

"Not exactly," Lucy said. "It's a big honor."

"But why us?" I asked. "Why now?" She explained to me that all the available chairs were taken, so Paco wanted to bump two of the padrinos out of their exalted seats before the altar in order to make room for us.

"He feels bad about us having to stand up for the whole ceremony," she added.

"That's very nice," I said, touched by the young man's thoughtfulness. "Tell him we accept."

"Being a padrino can be expensive," Lucy warned me.

"How expensive?"

"It's hard to say."

"Well," I said, "if it's going to cost more than fifty bucks, tell him we'd rather stand."

In the end, without a plausible excuse for refusing the honor (except that we were too cheap), we graciously accepted Paco's offer.

The ceremony, accompanied by lots of sweet-souled singing from an impromptu chorus, was, despite my inability to understand a single word, beautiful nonetheless. Babies and very small children crawled freely about on the floor throughout the entire Mass, which gave the proceedings a wonderfully natural and down-to-earth quality. Much to my delight, one child, who had somehow escaped his diapers, even peed on my shoe.

When the ceremony was over we all walked two blocks down the street to the house of Paco's parents. This, like most homes in Las Gardenias, was really a small ranchito, with a fenced-in vegetable garden, a miniature orchard and small enclosures for the livestock. The entire compound had been gaily decorated with brightly colored strings of *picapapel* (cutout paper squares), balloons and flowers.

Night had fallen now, and since Las Gardenias lacked electricity, our hosts had been obliged to procure a generator in order to provide illumination, and to power the four enormous speakers stacked up just inside the garden. Unhappily, this generator ran on gasoline and produced, along with the electricity, voluminous clouds of fumes and a sound not unlike that of an outboard motor revving up inside a shower stall.

But the noise from this generator, it turned out, was a mere whisper, like the sound of a feather falling, compared to the awesome, brain-crunching, *unbelievably* loud music which abruptly exploded forth like scratchy thunder from the titanic speakers.

The onset of this cacophony was the signal for the start of a series of beautifully quaint and typically Mexican customs. They began with a waltz, the bride and groom moving gracefully around the dusty yard as the several hundred guests applauded wildly. After a while, the couple broke off dancing in order to switch partners. The bride's new partner, after half a minute, took out a bill and pinned it onto her wedding gown. Across the yard, the woman who had been dancing with the groom did the same. Then they departed, to be replaced at once by another couple.

"What in the world is this?" I asked my wife.

"It's the *money dance*," she said. "Everybody takes turns dancing with the bride and groom and pinning money on their clothes."

"You're joking!" I said.

"It's no joke," she said. "No money dance, no honeymoon."

Several minutes later, a woman approached and handed each of us a pin. It was then I noticed that quite a few people were staring at us expectantly. With a heavy heart I fished two twenty dollar bills out of my wallet and handed one to my wife.

I've always been a spectacularly bad dancer, and when my turn came my ears began to burn with embarrassment. To make matters worse, there was a dramatic height differential to be reckoned with; I am only moderately tall, but the diminutive bride was almost as short as Dustin Hoffman. In order to hold my partner I was therefore forced to stoop grotesquely, making me look like the Hunchback of Notre Dame trying to tie his shoes.

When, after a few seconds of this torture, another man mercifully tapped me on the shoulder, I put the pin through the twenty-dollar bill and attempted to attach it to the dress. But I was never very good with pins. My shaking hand missed the mark entirely and I wound up sticking the tiny bride, who gave out a little yelp. In the end, she plucked the bill from my hand and pinned it on herself, as above the deafening blast of the music could clearly be heard the sound of the entire wedding party laughing uproariously at my ineptitude.

The money dance was followed by a curious ritual in which the groom put on an apron, picked up a broom and began to dance by himself all around the yard.

"Why is he dancing with a broom?" I shouted into my wife's ear.

"Quiet!" she shouted back," we're going to miss it."

"Miss what?"

Many of the groom's male friends and relatives gathered around him now, whistling, jeering and hurling insults. This activity went on for a surprisingly long time. I later learned that the entire business was supposed to symbolize the groom's imminent emasculation—something like a reverse Bar Mitzvah.

Then, suddenly, the groom swooned melodramatically into the arms of the same group of young men, who proceeded to pick him up and carry his limp body around the yard like a corpse. In the midst of the wild whoops, shouts and general hysteria which accompanied this puzzling spectacle, I turned to my wife and demanded an explanation.

"Now what are they doing?" I shouted.

"He died," she shouted back.

"I can see that he died," I said. "But what's the point?"

"How should I know?" my wife replied. "What do I look like, an encyclopedia?"

I never did precisely ascertain what this macabre custom was supposed to symbolize, though according to known authorities on the subject, it is in many ways reminiscent of infertility rites performed to this day in certain sections of New Jersey.

But I've forgotten the beer truck incident.

Halfway through the money dance a big beer truck pulled up to the front gate and Paco's father went out to talk to the driver. Then, hat in hand, he approached my wife and I and explained that since we were the padrinos of the beer, could we please fork over three hundred thousand pesos (around two hundred dollars at the time), so that he could pay the driver.

"Three hundred thousand pesos," I fumed. "Just to sit in a folding chair!"

"I warned you," my wife said.

"For two hundred dollars, I would've stood in the street," I moaned. "I would have stood on my head!"

In the end, I paid the driver, who gave me a terrible exchange rate, the entire amount in dollars.

With the arrival of the beer and the conclusion of the money dance and the mock funeral, the party really got under way. The lugubrious waltz was replaced by lively Ranchero music and soon everyone was laughing, hollering and kicking up their heels, and along with them an extraordinary amount of dust. Before long, all the dancers, including my wife and I, were covered from head to toe with a festive film of fine brown powder. But none of us minded in the least; we were having far too much fun.

Then someone handed me a bottle, and in the spirit of the occasion I took a healthy slug. It was Raicilla, a lighter fluid-like form of homemade liquor. After I got over the near-death experience of it napalming its way down to my stomach, I realized that this drano-esque beverage produced a rather pleasant effect. So I sought out the man with the bottle, who seemed to take an instant liking to me, and took another pair of painful pulls.

"That's Raicilla you're drinking," Lucy cautioned me. "You better take it easy. I don't think they're transplanting duodenums yet."

"Sure, baby, whatever you say," I said, swilling down some more.

As the party progressed, the dust, the fumes from the generator and the Liquid Plumber I had been imbibing set off a dangerously synergistic reaction in the vicinity of my brain, causing me to partially lose consciousness. As my awareness shriveled to the size of a sunflower seed, the only thought to which I could consistently cling centered on my need to find a bathroom.

Apparently there wasn't one, or else it was hopelessly occupied. So I sought out my Raicilla connection, with whom I had now established a strong fraternal bond, and the two of us, utilizing gestures which in other circumstances could have gotten us both arrested, held a short wordless conversation. Raoul—I believe that was his name—seemed to be telling me that I should wander off into the bushes and take care of my necessities there.

Dizzy, disoriented and, not to put too fine a point on it, drunk, I proceeded to do just that. Because I did not want to relieve myself too close to the festivities, I wound up wandering rather far afield, into areas of near-total darkness. Which was how, stumbling about uncertainly, I tripped over a low wooden fence and fell full-length into a pigsty.

For several moments I was unable to determine exactly what had happened to me. I spent this confused time rather unprofitably, I'm afraid, thrashing about in the muck like a beached fish. The pigs, meanwhile, startled by my abrupt entrance into their exclusive domain, began to make excited (possibly angry) snorting sounds. Visions of voracious man-eating swine tearing me to pieces flooded my imagination, which, along with the impressively disagreeable odor, impelled me to hurriedly navigate my way out of the pen and back toward the lights and sounds of the party.

Lumbering through the overgrowth, there was no way to ignore the fact that large portions of my person were now covered with what I tried to think of as mud, but knew deep in my heart to be sheer, undiluted pig slime. This knowledge naturally made me somewhat reluctant to rejoin the other guests.

So I circled cautiously around the party's perimeter until I spotted my wife.

"Oh my God!" she said. "What *happened* to you? You look like you've been swimming in pig shit."

"Never mind," I said. "Tell Paco and Irma I got sick. I'll meet you at the car."

At that moment, as my excremental luck would have it, Paco himself came trotting up to inform us that it was time to eat. Then, becoming aware of my unusual appearance, he said, "What happened to him?"

Holding her nose, my wife replied nasally, "It looks like he fell into a pigsty."

An utterly horrified expression transformed Paco's handsome young face as, holding his own nose, he grabbed my arm and began to yank me towards his house, nasally sobbing incomprehensible apologies.

"What's he saying?" I asked frantically. "Where's he taking me?"

"He's really upset," my wife said. "He's taking you to the bathroom so you can wash up."

"I don't want to wash up," I cried. "I want to leave."

Just as I was about to break free of Paco's surprisingly strong grip, his father came along, was informed of the situation and immediately grabbed his nose with one hand and my free arm with the other. Together, the two men, continuing to pinch their noses, escorted me forcibly across the yard, with my hysterically laughing wife trailing close behind. All around us, partygoers stopped what they were doing in order to stare at us with mystified expressions on their faces.

Struggling and cursing in English (which fortunately no one understood), I was dragged into the small house and up to the bathroom door, before which stood a long line of urologically-challenged individuals, all of whom had long ago ceased to feel any pain.

One look at me and the entire room full of people broke into unbridled laughter, catcalls and whistles. "I want to go home," I whimpered.

"Oh, come on, honey," my wife chided me, "you're the life of the party."

Whoever was inside the bathroom was taking an awfully long time. Soon everyone was holding their noses. Then people began to demand that I leave the room. Finally, Paco barged into the bathroom, removed its occupant, who had apparently fallen asleep, and dragged me inside. Lucy and Paco's father squeezed in behind us and secured the door.

With the four of us crowded into the tiny rustic bathroom, it was difficult to breathe and almost impossible to move. Paco, gagging and choking, attempted to wipe off my face with a tiny hand towel. His feeble but valiant efforts succeeded only in clogging both of my nostrils with pig slime. It soon became apparent that, short of stripping me naked in front of a fire-hose, there was little that could be done in the way of tidying me up. So I dove for the nearest exit.

Out of the house I ran, through the yard, past tables full of party-goers chewing chicken mole, past all of the neighbors in the street who hadn't been invited, but who were having their own party anyway, down the road and up to my car. All along the way I passed astonished looking people, all of whom began at once to sniff fearfully at the air, certain some environmental catastrophe had befallen their village.

Naturally, a small crowd was gathered around my car, why, I have no idea. In a moment I was joined by my wife who pointed out that it would not be wise in my current state to get inside the car. Then, as the incredulous on-lookers stared with their mouths agape, Lucy dug a pair of large black garbage bags out of the trunk. Poking a hole in the first bag she slipped it over my head. Then, poking two holes in the second bag, so that I would be able to walk, she slipped it over my feet and up to my waist.

"I'll drive," she said.

"Good idea," I said. "I've never driven with both my arms stuck inside a garbage bag before."

Halfway back to Vallarta, small round unidentified objects suddenly began to fly past our car. Then two of them smashed into the windshield and stuck there. Out of the corner of my eye, I noticed a garbage truck racing past us in the opposite direction.

"Pull over!" I screamed.

Parked safely on the side of the road, we inspected the windshield. The objects plastered against the glass turned out to be a pair of tortillas, which had struck our vehicle with a combined velocity of almost one-hundred and twenty miles an hour. Freeing an arm from the garbage bag, I attempted to peel them off with my fingers. But to no avail: due to the incredible force of the impact the tortillas had apparently fused with the glass.

As I stood there prying away futilely with my fingernails, saturated with super-viscous effluent and dressed from shoulder to ankle in hefty-sized garbage bags, a federal highway patrolman cruised to a halt behind our car. The policeman climbed cautiously out of his vehicle and approached, hand on holster, to within ten feet of where I was standing.

For a full minute the dismayed policeman stood staring silently at what had to be the first American he'd ever seen up close covered in pig filth and dressed in matching black plastic trash bags. On and on he stared, never uttering a word. Finally, I felt compelled to say something by way of explanation. So I pointed to the windshield and uttered one of the few Spanish words I could pronounce without difficulty.

"Tortillas," I said.

The policeman, apparently concluding that this was not a situation he wished to become involved in, shook his head, climbed back into his patrol car and sped away.

Having nothing better to do, I resumed clawing ineffectively away at the tortillas, while my wife resumed her fit of maniacal laughter.

It took my wife nearly a week to get over her giggling, and the birds in our yard even longer to finally peck away the last remnants of the tortillas from the windshield of our car.

Testing:
One, Two, Three…

Once many years ago, long before I moved to Mexico, my girlfriend, to whose title I had just affixed an "ex", called me a *parasite*. Since she had never provided me with anything in the way of financial support, I suppose she was attempting to say in a kind of general way that I was a lowly, disgusting and despicable organism which served no useful function and should, therefore, be exterminated. Or perhaps she was simply blowing off steam. Frankly, at the time I did not attach a great deal of significance to it; I was far too occupied attaching all of my available significance to her younger sister.

But then, many years later I moved to Mexico where I had the most frightening dream.

I dreamt that I was walking through a field of tall corn in the state of Iowa. I was naked, of course, and all the ears of corn had faces which were frowning at me with disapproval. Despite the apparent health of the corn, it was bone dry in the field and I was terribly thirsty. After trudging through the endless rows for what seemed like hours, I finally came upon a small pool of brackish water. As I bent to dip my fingers in the murky liquid, the tallest corn plant of them all suddenly shouted: "Stop! Don't do that!"

"Who are you?" I asked the plant, whose face bore a strong resemblance to my high school principal.

"I am the founder of the Republican Party," he announced in a booming voice.

On the instant, I was consumed with terror. The brackish water at my feet began to boil and to thicken until it had achieved the consistency of tar. Then small globules of steaming black goo began to separate themselves from the pool and to crawl toward me, splitting in half and multiplying with supernatural speed. Before I knew it, millions of tiny black gobs were crawling up my naked legs.

"What *are* these things?" I shouted desperately at the big corn plant, whose face now bore an eerie resemblance to James Brown.

"Good God!" the corn plant grunted, "Get Down! Soul Power!"

Then I awoke bathed in a cold sweat, which in the month of August in Puerto Vallarta is no mean feat.

Upon sober reflection I realized that my dream had not been about my neurotic fear of Republicans, but rather a thinly disguised expression of my anxiety over the fact that it was time to have my annual amoeba test.

Amoebas. Anyone who lives in a tropical or sub-tropical place like Puerto Vallarta must confront, sooner or later, the unpleasant possibility that these troublesome little creatures could have invaded their systems.

Amoebas are single-celled microorganisms, one of the oldest and most primitive forms of animal life still in existence. Like most Republicans, they shun conventional sex and reproduce by splitting themselves in half. Unfortunately, they do this with depressing regularity, which is a large part of the problem. Amoebas are parasites, which means that, like most politicians, they live off the labor of others. They come in a variety of species, but fall into three main categories: wimpy and harmless (liberal amoebas); dour and troublesome (conservative amoebas); vicious and virulent (radical right amoebas).

The harmless variety is content to remain in your alimentary canal, reproducing laconically and basically not bothering anyone.

The other two varieties, however, are real troublemakers. They reproduce at blinding speeds, draining your body of its hard-earned nutrients. Worse still, they eventually become bored with the digestive tract and begin to migrate to frighteningly unwholesome locations like the liver and the brain. Can you imagine anything more horrifying than having your whole brain filled to the brim with billions of bitsy Strom Thurmonds? Needless to say, these varmints must be dealt with promptly, mercilessly and with zero tolerance.

The standard, and some say, the only cure for amoebas is a truly noxious medicine called Flagyl. Flagyl, not to put too fine a point on it, is a poison. Its function is to kill everything inside your body without killing you. It often has unpleasant side effects and should not be taken without just cause. Unfortunately, all too often this is precisely what happens. The reason? People are too lazy or too squeamish to have themselves tested. Being tested twice a year is, according to most physicians, the prudent thing to do if you live in Mexico, or anywhere in the world with a similar latitudinal disposition.

What precisely is being tested? Well, in medical parlance, your *stool*. This is of course where the entire business becomes unpleasant and uncomfortable. Some people can barely bring themselves to talk about a stool analysis, let alone participate in one. This is, of course, a highly foolish attitude. Nature is nothing to be ashamed or frightened of. And what could be more natural than the act of moving one's bowels, or the albeit malodorous and organic material which exits the body via the posterior opening as a result of said act? If, as I know most of you believe, God created the world and everything in it, then He must also have, in His infinite wisdom, created shit. So then who are we humble humans to hold our noses as it were at Divine Creation?

Your personal responsibility in the analysis of your stool involves three steps: Production, Packaging and Delivery.

Producing a stool sample is, for most people, not a particularly difficult task, especially if one's daily diet includes a sufficient intake of fiber.

It is, therefore, in the Packaging phase of the operation where most people begin to experience a problem. What it all comes down to is this: How do you transfer an uncontaminated specimen of your caca into its sterilized container without making a mess or violating deeply rooted tribal taboos?

It just so happens that I have, over the years, perfected a completely fail-safe system for achieving just such an end. It is so simple and so easy that even a poorly coordinated child can use it. I call it the *Gerald Ford Procedure* (patent pending).

First, you will need to acquire the following: a roll of plastic Saran Wrap, a very clean plastic spoon and a sterilized container with a serious lid. Place all of these items within easy reach. Next, place your toilet-seat in a fully erect position. Then, cut off a three-foot length of Saran Wrap, and being sure to keep it dry, place it securely over the *mouth* of the toilet.

Hopefully at this point it will occur to you that stretching your saran wrap *tightly* over the mouth of the toilet may not be in your best interests. A certain amount of slack must be allowed in order to leave a comfortable space between the pitcher, as it were, and the catcher. This slack will prevent what folks in the trade refer to as *fecal feedback*.

Now some of you (those with a particularly strong aversion to the very notion of *fecal feedback*) will be tempted to overcompensate, leaving so much slack that the Saran Wrap actually comes into contact with the water at the bottom of the bowl. This is definitely not permissible, as it will contaminate the sample.

Once you have satisfactorily arrived at a nice spatial compromise vis-a–vis the Saran Wrap, you may lower the toilet seat, effectively locking your plastic "catcher's mitt" in place.

Now, have a seat, breathe deeply, remove all negative thoughts from your mind, and move your bowels.

Naturally, you will not want, during this phase of the procedure, to move your entire bowels. This would hopelessly weigh down the Saran Wrap, causing the whole ball of wax to wind up in the water, thus leaving you back at square one and with a messy logistical problem to boot.

Once you have assured yourself that there is indeed a tangible amount of analyzable material resting snugly in your stool stopper, rise to a quasi-upright position and grasp firmly your clean plastic spoon. Now, utilizing a cutting/scooping motion, detach a small amount of stool and deposit it carefully inside your sterilized container. If, as stool is sometimes wont to do, your specimen refuses to detach itself from the spoon no matter how hard you attempt to dislodge it, you may then be forced to pry it loose. If this is the case, be sure to use a sterile, disposable instrument.

Close the sterile container.

Now is the time to dispose of the spoon and the Saran Wrap in the most hygienic and efficient manner possible. I recommend depositing the spoon atop the Saran Wrap first. Then, lifting the toilet seat back to its upright position, gingerly grasp the Saran Wrap by its edges, fold it up and deposit the whole bundle in a waste paper basket.

Finally, if you feel the need to complete your bowel movement, go right ahead. And take your time. Your specimen has an unrefrigerated shelf life of up to three hours.

(Don't be alarmed, by the way, if your fresh specimen steams up the inside of its sterile container; this is completely normal and will not affect the validity of the analysis.)

Having successfully completed our Production and Packaging, it is now time for the Delivery, which is the soul of simplicity itself. Just place your sterile container in an *opaque* plastic bag (no sense in letting the neighbors know that you're walking around with a jar full of shit) and take it to the nearest laboratory.

At the laboratory explain to the person in charge (usually a young woman) that you are delivering a stool sample which you would like to have analyzed for the presence of amoebas. Don't feel embarrassed when she removes the container from its opaque plastic bag and stares at it thoughtfully for a moment. She is merely doing a quick "volume and freshness" check. And try to remember: to her, it's just a job.

The result of your test will either be "negativo" or "positivo". The latter means that you are indeed infected and must take your medicine. If your results are "negativo" you must deliver two more samples, hopefully on successive days, just to be sure. Amoebas are difficult to detect, and the "three strikes, they're out" rule is a good one to follow.

Well, that about wraps it up. Be sure to wash your hands with hot water and soap. And enjoy your next trip to the tropics.

A Tale Of Two Kidneys

Our maid, Berta, had the impassive chiseled face of a cigar store Indian and the body of a small NFL linebacker. She was a woman who was not afraid to speak her mind, and her choice of language often bordered on the lurid. As she stood there in the doorway of my bedroom leaning dourly on her broom, I could see that she had something on her mind. And whatever it was, like it or not, I was about to hear it.

"Son of a raped mother!" Berta barked at me, "I can't believe you're still in bed."

"It's my back, Berta," I said, emitting a convincing groan.

For three days now I'd been lying in bed gorging on aspirins and scalding myself with a heating pad turned up to the "meltdown" position. All, alas, to no avail.

"I don't think it's your stupid back," Berta announced solemnly. "I think it's your fucking kidneys."

"My kidneys?" I asked in alarm. "What makes you say that?"

Berta had given birth to seventeen children, fifteen of whom were still alive and borrowing (borrowing money from me at every opportunity): her off-the-cuff diagnoses were not, therefore, in my estimation, to be taken lightly.

"Your complexion," she said, eyeing me critically, "looks kidneyish."

"What?"

"And take that piece of shit off your back." She meant the heating pad. "I swear (before God and the Virgin of Guadalupe), you smell like a burning pork chop!"

Later that day when my wife returned from work, the first thing she said to me was: "You're still in bed."

"What a coincidence," I began, "you're the second person…"

"I hope you realize," Lucy went on, "that you're about to lose your job."

"I know," I told her. "But it won't be on account of absenteeism."

"No?"

"No. I'll be fired due to my dietary habits. The minute the sales manager finds out I'm a vegetarian, I'm as good as gone."

"What are you talking about?"

"The man's insane," I explained. "Last week, in the middle of one of his sadistic motivational meetings, he essentially ordered us to eat raw meat for breakfast. He told us we were a bunch of wimps, that the *ups*—that's what he calls the clients—were walking all over us, that we needed to be more aggressive, more determined, 'like Rocky Balboa'. Then he says, 'I don't know about you, but when I look in the mirror every morning, I see a hungry tiger'. And I believe it. Once, I actually heard him growling in the men's bathroom. The man is dangerous, honey. He belongs on a leash!"

"But I thought he liked you," Lucy said.

"He does," I replied. "That's the scary part."

My wife began to laugh.

"Speaking of scary," I went on, "Berta thinks there's something wrong with my kidneys. She says she can tell by my complexion. What do you think?"

Lucy leaned over and carefully examined my face. "Yeah, it is kind of a weird color," she said.

"What color?"

"Well, it's hard to say. Yellowish-green, I guess."

"Yellowish-green!" I shouted. "What do you mean, yellowish-green?"

"You know," Lucy said, "like vomit. Hey, do you smell something burning?"

The next morning I found myself sitting in the office of an obese man with beady pig-like eyes who claimed to be a urologist. His name was Dr. Garcia Garcia, which is not a typographical error. In Mexico everyone has two last names—the last name of one's father, followed by the last name of one's mother. When people with two common names such as Garcia or Martinez marry each other, these odd sounding double-names are then bestowed upon their unfortunate children.

If Dr. Garcia Garcia was indeed a specialist, he would have been the first to practice medicine in Puerto Vallarta. In defense of my adopted home I should probably mention that these events took place in the town's deep dim past when running water and electricity were still considered by many to be works of the devil, when burros outnumbered automobiles and when the greater Puerto Vallarta area contained only a single traffic light, which everyone ignored.

As a matter of fact, I did not have to rely on Dr. Garcia Garcia's word alone that he was a bona-fide medical specialist. All around me were clues which led ineluctably to that conclusion. First, there was the desk, so large you could have landed a small airplane on it. So large that there was no way it could have fit through the doorway. In all likelihood the room had been built around it. Then there was Dr. Garcia Garcia's outfit, one of those white polyester smocks with all the buttons down one side. Dressed in that fashion he had to be either a doctor or a barber, and I didn't see any combs.

Even the walls told anyone who cared to look upon them that they were in the presence of a serious urologist. Not one, but two giant full-color posters of the male uro-genital tract adorned these walls, which were in serious need of some fresh paint. The posters were very similar, differing only in their interpretation of the male bladder. In one poster the bladder looked like an inflated lima bean; in the other, like a Polish sausage.

Dr. Garcia Garcia was not a man to waste time on pleasantries. "What's your problem?" he demanded at once.

I explained about the persistent pain in my lower back. He nodded once and produced from a drawer in his desk a very small plastic cup. It was, in fact, much smaller than a Dixie-cup, though somewhat larger than the little paper catsup containers they used to give you at fast-food restaurants. Handing me the cup, he gave me terse directions to the bathroom.

"Doctor," I asked reluctantly, "don't you have anything a little larger?"

"No," he said.

Twenty minutes later I was seated once again at the behemoth desk. Though he did not appear to have it on his person at that precise moment, I assumed that the doctor was by now aware of the contents of my specimen. Apparently, I was not mistaken.

"You have a kidney infection," he informed me with brutal directness. Then, whipping out a prescription pad, he said, "It's easily treatable. In a week you will be perfectly fine."

Not until the pharmacist had handed me three separate boxes did my feeling of euphoric relief begin to evaporate. Why three?

Back at the house I took out my giant red PDR and proceeded to look up the three medicines. They were all antibiotics and all of them were deemed to be effective in the treatment of, among other things, kidney infections. But why three?

After thinking it over I came to the conclusion that Dr. Garcia Garcia must be operating under what is called the "Infinity Assumption". This clever proposition was created in an attempt to put a friendly face on a pair of uncomfortably inaccessible concepts: *infinity* and *eternity*. It goes something like this: If you placed an infinite number of chimpanzees in front of an infinite number of typewriters, eventually one of the chimps would write *Hamlet*. Or, if you placed an infinite number of lawyers and time-share salesmen in front of an infinite number of clients, eventually one of them would say something which was *true*.

Finally, I closed the PDR and swallowed the first three pills along with my reservations.

Seven days later, I had faithfully ingested all of my medication and the pain in my back had not diminished in the least.

"I'm not surprised," Dr. Garcia Garcia informed me, after I had explained to him the current state of my renal affairs.

"You're not?" I asked the man who had told me that in seven days I would be "perfectly fine".

Reaching into one of the cavernous desk drawers, Dr. Garcia Garcia removed an enormous syringe and proceeded to load it with the contents of three separate vials.

"I guess those are vitamins?" I asked the reticent doctor.

Garcia Garcia frowned and continued to load the syringe.

"What's in the vials, doctor?" I persisted.

"I am going to give you an injection every day for the next five days," he said, ignoring my question yet again.

"An injection of what?" I demanded.

"Antibiotics," he replied tersely.

"Which antibiotics?"

Dr. Garcia Garcia glared malevolently at me and said nothing.

"Would they happen to be the same ones I've just finished taking?" I asked.

"Of course," he said, his tone reeking with condescension.

"Garcia," I said, dropping the family name of his mother (or his father) as well as his professional title, "let me tell you two things, you bloated egotistical quack. Number one, you are *not* going to inject me every day for the next five days. Number two…"

"How dare you!" Garcia Garcia shouted with an utter lack of imagination as he lurched to his feet.

After an instant's reflection, I realized that there was no real percentage in getting into "number two", so I hastily left the premises before the irate croaker could waddle around his immense desk and throttle me.

I spent most of the next day laying in bed waiting for my wife to return with news of my airline reservations: in three days time I was supposed to fly to San Francisco to see a real urologist. Around noon, Berta, looking especially solemn, poked her Mt. Rushmore head into the room and told me that before I threw my hard-earned money away flying to the U.S. (naturally it could be put to better use by her children), I should go to see a homeopath right here in Puerto Vallarta.

"What the hell's a homeopath?" I asked suspiciously. "Is that like a psychopath? Some kind of gay serial killer?"

"A homeopath is a doctor," Berta explained patiently, "who uses natural medicines. When a regular doctor, like the male whore you went to, can't help, then you go to a homeopath."

"What do you mean by natural medicines?" I asked.

"Herbs," Berta replied. "Herbs and…whatever."

I liked the idea of herbs. At worst, they were harmless. But I was not entirely, altogether certain about the *whatever*. As luck would have it, the particular homeopath Berta had in mind turned out to be a devoted dispenser of *whatever*.

Dr. Hernandez Fernandez (not a double-name, but close) was a good deal more cordial, and less corpulent than his predecessor, Dr. Garcia Garcia. On the other hand, the two doctors did have a disquieting number of things in common.

The homeopath's desk was, if anything, even larger than that of the bogus urologist. And he too was wearing one of those oddly buttoned polyester garments. The homeopath even had two large nearly identical color posters on the walls of his office, though neither, thank God, contained a bladder. Each poster depicted a giant human eyeball, one clearly marked "left", and one "right". Emanating from the irises of each eye were dozens of lines which in turn pointed to words on the margins of the posters. Words such as *ear*, *feet*, *brain*, *lungs*, and so on.

Dr. Hernandez Fernandez, with the graciousness of a true caballero, asked me to describe my problem, which I did. Throughout my long sad story, he gave me his sincere and undivided attention. When I had finished, he drew his chair alongside mine and took my wrist gingerly between his thumb and forefinger. He was, I was delighted to see, taking my pulse, which was a damned sight more than the so-called urine-man had done.

Sixty seconds later Dr. H. F. was still taking my pulse, and I began to experience serious doubts relating to the entire situation. The svelte homeopath, it seemed to me, had entered into a kind of trance. His eyes had closed, his breathing had slowed and a faint smile had pasted itself upon the delicate lips of his finely featured face, as if he were reliving some long ago childhood trip to Disneyland, or to the Turkish Baths.

Another full minute passed, and just as I was about to reclaim my wrist and bolt for the exits, the doctor's eyes snapped open and he emitted a deep satisfied grunt. Then, releasing my wrist, he produced a loupe and proceeded to examine my eyes from extremely close range (had he been any closer he would have been in my lap). This examination also went on for an uncomfortably long time. But when finally I could stand it no longer, when I was on the verge of handing the man a month-to-month lease, Dr. Hernandez Fernandez withdrew himself and the loupe from my proximity and emitted satisfied grunt number two.

Returning nimbly to his side of the titanic desk, he busied himself making notes for a while. Then he spent some time gathering his wits and steepling his fingers.

"Your *urologist,*" he finally said, pronouncing the word with utter disdain, "was correct about one thing: you do have a kidney infection. In ten days, however, you will be completely cured. Come this way."

Dr. Hernandez Fernandez had dropped his charming beside manner and was now all business as he led me to a small cubicle, sat me down and handed me a dish containing ten tiny lumpy white pills. "Take these," he ordered. "I'll be right back."

Five minutes later, true to his word the doctor returned and said, "How do you feel?"

"What do you mean?" I replied. The homeopath's question made no sense to me. Only five minutes had passed since I had taken the pills. What was supposed to happen in five minutes? Was I supposed to faint? Attain Nirvana? Grow a third testicle?

Dr. H.F. did not appear to comprehend the cause of my confusion. "I mean," he said impatiently, "how do you feel?"

"Fine," I replied, wondering frantically what the hell he was getting at.

"Good," he said, handing me another ten itty-bitty pills. Take these."

When he returned several minutes later, I was determined to answer his question intelligently, no matter how stupid it made me appear.

"How do you feel now?" he asked anxiously.

"Doctor, do you mean, how do I feel since I took the pills? Is that what you are asking me?"

"Yes, yes. Of course," he replied.

"The same," I said.

"The same as what?" he asked nervously.

"The same as I did before I took the pills," I replied, feeling even more like a moron.

"Good." He seemed relieved. Why, I had no idea.

When he handed me the next round of lumpy little balls I popped them right into my mouth, just to demonstrate that, even if I was too much of an idiot to decipher his mysterious questions, I was at least docile enough to promptly follow his bizarre instructions.

When I had consumed forty of the little pills and still showed no signs of whatever it was the homeopath seemed to fear, I was treated to one final grunt, which to my increasingly paranoid ear contained more notes of relief in it than it did of satisfaction.

Finally, Dr. Hernandez Fernandez handed me four vials full of the little white pills with instructions as to when and how many to consume. Then he charged me the equivalent of two dollars and sent me on my way—but not before I had convinced him to write out for me the names of whatever it was he had been dosing me with.

Back at the house I rushed to my Petite LaRousse dictionary and unfolded the scrap of paper Dr. H.F. had given me. Four words were written there in Spanish. Three of them looked frighteningly familiar. When translated into English, they turned out to be, just as I had feared, *arsenic, mercury* and *sulfur*. The fourth word, the unfamiliar one, was *lead*.

Marching straight away to the bathroom I deposited, first the contents of the four vials, and then the remnants of my lunch into the appropriate receptacle: So much for natural medicine.

The urologist in San Francisco reminded me of an ill-tempered vulture. He was tall, thin, unnaturally pale and had that buzzard-like stoop about his neck and shoulders. Aside from that, he was not a particularly pleasant man. Maybe he had poked his nose up into one too many bladders, or down into one too many urine samples. Whatever the cause, he simply radiated disgust: disgust with me, with himself, with my x-rays, my lab results and the whole world in general.

"You have *no* infection," he informed me, his voice dripping with impatience and irritation. "You've had *no* infection," he added as if this fact were somehow my fault. "What you *do* have are several large stones lodged in your kidneys."

"Stones?"

"Yes. Just like little chunks of Mt. Vesuvius," he said, curling his lip in a miserable attempt at a smile.

"So what do I *do* about it?" I asked, giving the repulsive creature a dose of his own medicine.

"Drink a lot water and hope for the best," he replied indifferently. "See the receptionist on your way out."

The receptionist wore a frozen smile so phony it looked as if it had just been glued onto her face. From beneath a kilo of makeup she informed me cheerfully, "That will be five-hundred dollars."

Five hundred dollars!

In Mexico I had been verbally abused, misdiagnosed, misprescribed and poisoned. But I'd had to fly all the way to California in order to be mugged.

The Hotel Enigma

Frau Himmler, the owner and sole proprietress of the Hotel Enigma, was a huge fan of the occult. Possessed to no small degree of that notorious "Old World Charm", she struck me as a perfect cross between Leona Helmsly and Count Dracula.

My acquaintance with the Teutonic Hotelier was short and bittersweet, and has left upon me a deep impression to this day.

How Frau Himmler came to reside in the charming lakeside resort of Valle de Bravo in the State of Mexico, I was unable to ascertain. Our first and only real conversation touched mainly on more topical matters.

"You will not find an empty room anywhere else in this whole town," she told me in heavily accented, but otherwise excellent English.

This was true. I had made the mistake of arriving in Valle de Bravo on a Saturday. During the week Valle was just another quiet Mexican town. On the weekends, however, it filled, then overflowed with "Chilangos" (a mildly derogatory term for residents of Mexico City) all desperate to escape the smog-bound, crime-ridden, traffic-jammed nightmare of their collective day to day existence.

Valle de Bravo had a total of five hotels, and as Frau Himmler had claimed, hers was the only one with a single vacancy. This fact alone should have made me suspicious, but I was feeling a little desperate myself at the moment, and Frau Himmler was *very* persuasive.

"These are not mere rooms," she declared triumphantly as she handed me a poorly photocopied sheet listing "Services and Amenities". "I have only three-room suites," she continued, "with fully equipped kitchens. My staff is highly professional—trained by me personally. Each suite contains a small library with books in four languages. Have you ever read the works of Alistair Crowley, by the way?"

"Tell me," I said, anxious to change the subject, "do you have safe deposit boxes here?"

Frau Himmler flinched, as if she had been slapped in the face, then snorted with disdain, "Young man, Valle de Bravo is a serene, peaceful town. The people here are warm, open, friendly and completely honest. Crime is virtually unknown. You have no need for a lock box in *this* establishment."

"I'm sorry. I didn't mean to imply..."

"How long will you be staying with us?"

Frau Himmler's timing was excellent. She had chosen the perfect moment to go for the close. I wondered briefly if she had ever sold time-share.

"Oh, I'm not sure," I said feebly, "four or five days, I suppose."

"Excellent. Then I can give you our special four or five day discount: Fifty percent off."

"That seems reasonable. I..."

"Shortly, I will be leaving for Mexico City on urgent business. I must have the full amount in advance."

"Well, I guess I..."

"Cash only, please. I do not accept credit cards."

The key to my suite was attached to a large flat block of wood the size of a ping pong paddle, thereby rendering it both impossible to misplace and extremely difficult to use. The door to my suite was on the ground floor and faced a cheery little garden filled with flowers and fruit trees. Using both hands I managed to insert the key in the lock and turn it twice without bruising my knuckles.

The door opened inward, which was not terribly unusual, but in the case of the Hotel Enigma, unwise, since something inside the room was preventing the door from opening fully. Being slender, I had no problem squeezing inside, but I was forced to insert my suitcase separately.

At first glance I seemed to be in an entry way, a foyer the size of a large closet. But this large closet contained a two-burner stove, a miniature refrigerator, a tiny table with two chairs and a shallow sink, forcing me to the unwelcome conclusion that I was now standing in the "fully equipped kitchen".

In the far corner of this tiny room there was an unbelievably narrow spiral staircase which I would soon discover was the only means of achieving access to the remainder of the suite.

Risking serious vertebral dislocation, I stepped side-ways onto the first rung. Then, twisting myself into a hideously contorted position, I attained step number two.

At this point I glanced up, relieved to see that I did not have far to go. Fortunately the rooms were low-ceilinged and the spiral staircase to hell had only eight rungs.

Twisting, slouching, crouching and crunching, I finally reached the second floor. This was the bedroom and it was even smaller than the kitchen, due to the fact that it also housed the bathroom. I glanced quickly down at the bed: visibly sagging, it was smaller than a twin but larger than a casket.

I decided to push on. There was one more room to go and I was hoping Frau Himmler had saved the best for last.

She hadn't.

The third floor was another minuscule cube with an even lower ceiling, a small television, a bookcase, a sliding glass door and an imitation naugahide armchair. The room must have been built around the armchair since there was no way it could have been schlepped up the stairs.

What with the books, the television and the chair, I decided that this must be the "entertainment center". I also decided that I'd rather sleep inside my car than inside this torture chamber (there was more legroom in the car).

Descending the stairs proved to be even more difficult than climbing up them. I finally decided to pretend I was a snake and simply slither down.

My suitcase was exactly where I had left it. Frau Himmler, on the other hand, was nowhere to be found. I would have knocked on her door just to be sure, but it was guarded by an enormous snarling Doberman who was tied to the doorknob by a ten-foot chain. Next to the front door was a sign which read in bold blood-red letters: VICIOUS DOG ON DUTY 24 HOURS A DAY. SPECIAL SECURITY SYSTEMS. SPECIAL ALARMS. TRESPASSERS WILL BE PROSECUTED!

Frau Himmler's 1943 Volkswagen Bug was nowhere to be found, either, so apparently I was not going to get my money back My erstwhile hostess had flown the coop and in record time. She was probably in Argentina by now, living under an assumed name and selling gold fillings door to door.

Valle de Bravo is surrounded by gently rolling pine-covered hills which are perfect for hiking, and a large serene lake ideal for boating. And so I spent my first two days hiking, boating and performing yoga exercises in a vain attempt to counteract the insidious effects of the spiral staircase, not to mention the bed, sleeping on which constituted a form of cruel and unusual punishment even Amnesty International would have found difficult to digest.

On the evening of the second day it began to rain. The next morning it was raining solid sheets of water. Leaving the suite was out of the question. Fortunately I had purchased some provisions against this eventuality, and so I began to make myself breakfast.

Making and eating breakfast proved to be something of an experience. First I put some margarine into the nineteenth century frying pan. Then I lit the left burner of the stove, causing the minute room to instantly fill with noxious fumes. I rushed to open the window, which was located conveniently next to the stove. A wet blast of air came rushing in, which did not immediately blow out the flame. Before that it helpfully blew the cheerful curtains over the top of the stove where they began to catch fire.

I closed the window and opened the door. This allowed a not inconsiderable amount of water into the room, but it was a vast improvement over being asphyxiated and/or burned alive.

When my scrambled eggs and toast were ready, I began to investigate how best to sit at the cramped table, a maneuver I had not ventured to attempt until now.

There were two chairs. One of these was so close to a wall that it could only be sat in sideways, which made eating off of the table somewhat awkward. The other chair allowed you to sit actually facing the table, but its position left one no alternative but to plant one's feet squarely atop the head of a long-dead lion.

I had heard of bear skin rugs before. I may even have seen one once. But a lion skin rug? Replete with head and tail? This was something new to my experience. Poor Simba covered most of the kitchen floor, making him by far the largest object in the entire suite. Where Frau Himmler had procured a lion from and why she had decided to install it on the kitchen floor, I did not even want to hazard a guess.

Breakfast over, it was time to attend to my morning toiletries.

The bathroom was a model of efficient design. In fact, once inside this architectural marvel, the need for lateral movement was almost completely eliminated. The micro-sink as well as the imported toilet were both located entirely within the confines of the shower stall. This enabled me to perform various bodily functions, brush my teeth and take a shower all at the same time.

On the morning of my fourth and final quality day in Valle de Bravo, it was still raining non-stop and harder than ever. I had made several forays into the outside world to stock up on supplies and grab a few meals, but there really wasn't a whole lot else to do. Boating on the lake was, of course, unthinkable. Hiking would have been suicidal. Even going for a short drive was a risky proposition since visibility even at high noon was nearly non-existent.

So I sat in the puke-green imitation naugahide easy chair on the third floor and went slowly insane.

When a person goes insane he or she is liable to do strange things. One of the strange things I did was to take out the Hotel Enigma's official photocopied list of "Services and Amenities" and make an in-depth analysis of how it coincided with reality.

The list included the following: Fully equipped kitchen. Television. Telephone with free, unlimited local calls. Small multi-lingual library. Daily maid service. Balcony with breath taking views.

I began my survey from top to bottom.

First, I turned on the TV. It was of sub-atomic size, of course, black and white and almost received one station. Minus fifteen points for Frau Himmler.

Next I opened the "sliding" glass doors and, braving the rain, attempted to step out onto the ungenerous balcony. This proved to be more than a little difficult. It was necessary to both duck and suck in my stomach at the same time, which still left my buttocks inside the room. As for the view...minus twenty points.

The mini-library did indeed contain books in four different languages. Oddly enough, none of them were English or Spanish. Minus five points.

Twisting and deforming myself down to the second floor, I attempted to reach the telephone. This antique device (the last time I had seen a phone like this was on re-runs of *Hogan's Heroes*) had been strategically placed so that the only way to lay one's hands on it was by lying across the midget-sized bed. This I proceeded to do. When I picked up the receiver to make the first of my free unlimited local calls, there was of course no dial tone. Minus twenty-five points.

Next I proceeded to serpentine down to the kitchen where the words "fully-equipped" took on a whole new meaning. Minus ten points.

Last but not least was the daily maid service. The maid did indeed come every day. She must have been at least a hundred and twenty years old and for her the spiral staircase might as well have been Mt. McKinley. She wisely limited her activities to cleaning the kitchen, depositing a change of linen on the table and berating me for leaving scuffmarks on the lion's head.

Minus fifteen points.

Out of a possible score of 100 points on the truth in advertising scale, Frau Himmler had lurched into last place with a dismal ten points.

The following morning I was all packed up and ready to drive to Mexico City where I planned to visit some friends, have myself injected with lethal doses of liquid valium and try to unwind.

As I loaded my car I noticed that Frau Himmler's black Volkswagen was back in its usual spot. Seeing Frau Himmler before I left was high on my list of priorities, as there were several impressions I wished to share with her. Also, I had filled the back of the "Services and Amenities" list with my point by point analysis and desired very much to hand it to her personally.

Naturally, it had now stopped raining. The Doberman was nowhere to be seen—probably being fed large hunks of horseflesh so as to render him marginally more docile for the weekend rush.

Walking boldly up to the door, I knocked briskly. Nothing. I knocked again, and felt the entire structure shake as thirty-five kilos of maddened canine launched itself against the other side of the door. Between guttural blood-curdling growls and rabid insidious snarls, I yelled out Frau Himmler's name.

Nothing but more snarls and growls. I waited a full minute and shouted out her name again.

"What is it?" Her voice sounded impatient and annoyed from the other side of the door.

"I'd like to speak with you for a minute," I yelled.

"I'm busy."

"It'll only take a second," I screamed as the incensed Dobbie continued to assault the door.

"Come back later," she said dismissively.

"I can't. I'm leaving right now."

"I'm very busy," she replied through the door.

"Alright," I yelled, rolling up the Services and Amenities list and wedging it between the door handle and the jamb. "I just wanted to tell you that I had the phone repaired while you were gone and I made a few calls to California. I'll send you a check."

"What!"

By the time the dog had been secured and the door opened, I was already inside my car. As Frau Himmler charged the passenger door, I floored the gas pedal, popped the clutch and blew a small kiss to a woman I hoped very much never to see again.

Mummy Dearest

The nephew from hell turned-up at my beach house in Puerto Vallarta, as threatened, on a horribly hot, muggy day in the month of June. Tall and gawky, twenty years old (and going on twelve), sullen, morbid and addicted to video games, Martin and I had so little in common it was difficult to believe that we belonged to the same species, let alone the same family.

Nothing interested or excited this strange young man. The jungle was boring. Dolphins he had seen already—on TV. Swimming in the ocean was far too much effort. In fact, the only time he displayed any animation whatsoever was when we had driven past the scene of a serious automobile accident. For fifteen minutes he had begged me to turn around so we could inspect the carnage with the thoroughness it deserved.

Then it rained, a true tropical deluge which lasted for hours and hours.

The first serious rain of the season always flushes hordes of land crabs out of their holes in the sand surrounding my house. Land crabs are truly ludicrous looking things who walk sideways on their tiptoes and who wear their eyes on the ends of short batons. Somehow, despite all the screened-in doors and windows, they manage to insinuate themselves into every corner of the house. For myself, even though they display an annoying affinity for the insides of shoes, I like the crabs. They make me laugh. My cat is fond of them, too. Unable to either eat or maim them, she loves to bat them around the tile floors like hockey pucks.

My nephew's attitude towards these inoffensive creatures was, to put it politely, psychopathic.

"Is it all right if I stomp on one?" he asked me that evening with a chilling matter-of-factness.

"Why do you want to do that?" In the course of that long day I had for some reason begun to assume with my nephew the detached tone and manner of a clinical psychiatrist.

Martin shrugged his narrow, permanently hunched shoulders. "There's hundreds of them," he said, "what difference does it make?"

"Oh, I'm not worried about them becoming an endangered species," I said. "I'm just curious: do you often get the urge to crush the life out of living things with your feet?"

"Well can I or can't I?" my nephew demanded.

"Be my guest," I said. "Just do it outside."

While Martin was out in the dark garden, I decided that it would probably be wise to lock up the steak knives before I went to bed that night. But before I could take any action, he was back, to ask if I would hold the flashlight while he "crushed a few".

"Look," I said serenely, "if you want to commit genocide against the entire land crab population of Puerto Vallarta, I won't try to stop you. But I'm not going to help you either."

"Then I guess I'll go to bed," he said dejectedly, as if sleep were the only viable alternative to an evening of crabicide.

Martin's murderous impulses having been momentarily thwarted, he segued smoothly the following morning into an obsession with base instinct number two: sex.

"So, uncle," he demanded as he stuffed his face with quesadillas, "when am I going to get laid?"

This was the morning of day three, our third consecutive breakfast together. Unfortunately for me, my wife was out of town and all of the domestic duties were falling upon my reluctant shoulders. Martin naturally hadn't the vaguest idea how to prepare food for himself.

"When?" I repeated stupidly.

"Yeah, when. That's what I said."

"I'm sure I don't know," I said. "Should we get out the Ouija board?"

"What I meant," Martin said with the frayed patience of a busy man who is forced to explain something self-evident to a hopeless idiot, "is when are you going to introduce me to a cute girl?"

"Oh."

"So that I can get laid."

"Well, let's see," I said, deftly trading in my psychotherapist's cap for that of an obliging pimp. "Was there any particular type of cute girl you had in mind?"

"Yeah," he said, "between eighteen and twenty-one. Good body. Pretty face. Mexican—I definitely want a Mexican. And she has to speak English."

"Right," I said. "She has to understand you when you tell her to take off her pants."

"Right," my nephew agreed.

"Now then," I went on, "when we say 'good body', are we talking about the typical North American Barbie Doll configuration?"

"What?"

"Big tits and small waist," I explained.

"Of course."

"Well, I don't see any problem there," I told my nephew, "but you'll have to wait until Aunt Lucy gets home."

"Aunt Lucy?"

"Yes, you know, my wife?"

"What has she got to do with it?" Martin demanded testily, which gave me a small brief ray of hope for the family gene pool; this was the first intelligent question he had asked me since his arrival.

My wife, inconveniently up in California visiting her mother, was the family director for social interaction. In fact, she had a real talent for match making, and if there was anyone (beside Jane Goodall) who could find a potential mate for my nephew, it was Lucy.

But I explained it a little differently to Martin. "Martin," I said, "if I am going to go prowling around Puerto Vallarta with you looking for cute young Mexican girls between the ages of eighteen and twenty-one, I'm going to need my wife along for protection."

"Protection against what?"

"Divorce for starters," I said. "And bodily disfigurement, eternal poverty, murder—you know, that sort of thing."

"I don't understand," Martin said. "Who's gonna murder you?"

So much for the family gene pool.

Lucy wasn't due home for another five days, so Martin and I spent this "down-time", as he called it, getting to know each other better—an experience which ranked somewhere between dengue fever and prostate cancer on the family fun scale.

My nephew's typical day-on-vacation began at a little before noon, when he immerged from bed. What followed, the first thirty minutes of Martin's waking existence, was not a pretty sight and one from which I did my best to remain aloof.

Once he had attained a sufficiently realized degree of consciousness, one which enabled him to perform the function of speech, he would approach me and say, "When's breakfast?"

I made my nephew quesadillas every day. I did this because they were quick, easy, clean and nutritious. The quesadilla is in fact so quick and easy to prepare that even a chimpanzee, or a registered Republican, could probably be trained to make one.

My nephew, of course, could never seem to get the hang of it.

When breakfast was over Martin realized that he was out of cigarettes.

"Could you go get me some cigarettes?" he asked.

I told him that he could probably go get them himself.

"But I don't speak Spanish," he complained.

I explained to my nephew that mastery of the Spanish language was not a prerequisite for buying a pack of cigarettes in Puerto Vallarta.

"So what do I do?" he asked.

"I suggest you enter a liquor store, approach the counter and say, 'Marlboro'."

"And they'll know what I'm talking about?"

Incredibly enough, my nephew returned twenty minutes later empty handed. He had followed all of my instructions to the letter, except for the one about approaching the counter. He had stood, he told me, for five minutes (an eternity for him) in the middle of the store where person after person had walked around him and been attended to.

"They wouldn't wait on me," he said.

"That's because you didn't walk up to the counter," I told him.

"Up to the counter?"

Later that afternoon we took a long but pleasant drive to the northern tip of the bay, Punta de Mita, a long, wind-swept shell-filled beach, which abounds in sea birds and spectacular views.

We had been out of the car and walking along the beach for almost five minutes when Martin turned to me and said, "Ready?"

"Ready for what?" I asked.

"Ready to leave," he said impatiently.

"But we just got here," I protested.

"So?"

This scene was to be repeated over and over again as I took my nephew to all of the wonderful rivers, jungles and beaches in and around Puerto Vallarta. No matter how extraordinary and beautiful the surroundings, five minutes in any one location was his absolute limit.

Finally, I was forced to the conclusion that my nephew was not a "nature person". This fact, coupled with his incessant whining and pleading that I take him to the Hard Rock Café, led me, on the evening before my wife's return, to do just that.

Once again it was raining with Old Testament intensity as we set out in the family Volkswagen down Avenida Mexico, the main street in town, which had been for the moment converted into a small river with miniature rapids at every intersection. Though picturesque as they come, Avenida Mexico, from an engineering standpoint, left more than a little to be desired. The charmingly rustic cobblestones which have always lined all of Vallarta's streets, were still several years away from being cemented down and any strong rain tended to loosen them. Which explains at least partly how the front left tire of my car came to lodge itself inside a two-foot deep ditch several blocks before our destination. Extricating the poor Bug proved to be impossible and so we were forced to abandon the vehicle there for the night and cover the remaining two blocks on foot.

The interior décor of the Hard Rock Café never did a great deal for me but it was, I had to admit, filled with lots of nubile young prospects, many of whom were as soaking wet as ourselves. I ordered a couple of Coronas and we stood at the bar, sipping on our beers. Directly across from us, no more than eight feet away, were three tender babes sitting at a railing, their young resilient breasts wonderfully highlighted by the soaked translucent fabric of their blouses.

"Well," I told my nephew, "there you go."

"Where?"

"The girls," I said.

"What about them?"

"What about them? They're young, cute, sopping wet and unattended. What more do you need to know?"

"I don't know," he said.

"You don't know what?" I demanded.

My nephew finished his beer, looked around distractedly for a minute and said, "Ready?"

When my wife got home the next day I had a few choice words for her.

"How could you do this to me?" I whined. "Leaving me in the lurch with my nephew for over a week! It's cruel, is what it is."

My wife began to laugh.

"What's so funny?" I cried.

"That's just who your nephew reminds me of," she said.

"Who?"

"Lurch: the butler on *The Munsters*. Or was it *The Adams Family*?"

"Never mind that," I told her. "We have more pressing matters. You've got to find him a girlfriend right away."

"A girlfriend?" Lucy said.

"Yes."

"You mean, like a female primate?"

"Precisely."

"No problem," Lucy said uncertainly. My wife loved a challenge...up to a point.

That very same evening as the clock struck midnight the three of us piled into the car and headed for *The Zoo*. This was the place we had concluded, after much checking around, most likely to contain a potential breeding partner for my nephew.

The Zoo was one of those clubs for young people which played unbearably loud recorded music in a pathetic attempt to create a wild, anything-goes type ambiance. The idea, if you were one of those unfortunately repressed young patrons, was to get disgustingly drunk, jump around like an idiot, make loud animal noises and lose most if not all of your civilized inhibitions. In keeping with the wildlife theme, there were even a pair of large cages into which young ladies were encouraged to place themselves and, once inside, move about with the wild and anguished abandon of cats in heat.

As I say, it appeared to be the ideal place for my nephew.

By just after midnight *The Zoo* was packed with a nice blend of young Mexican, American and Canadian savages. The air was thick with cigarette smoke, bad rock and roll, nausea inducing strobe lights and the combined scent of a dozen cheap perfumes and roll-on deodorants. While I rushed to the bar to numb my battered sensibilities, Lucy grabbed Martin's arm and together they began to troll the room.

Fishing, no matter how skillful the fisherman, always contains a large element of luck. On this night at least, my nephew's luck was truly extraordinary.

I barely had time to finish my second shot of tequila when Lucy, Martin and two young women joined me at the crowded bar. One young lady I recognized as the daughter of Lucy's manicurist. She was a nice girl, but unsuitably short and plump. Her friend, on the other hand, was something else entirely. She was tall for a Mexican, slender, exceedingly pretty and dressed to create havoc. Though not Barbie-class, her mammarys did project outward at a pleasingly pert angle and were only marginally contained by just the hint of a red tank top. She appeared to be about twenty years old and spoke excellent English.

"Where are you from, Talia?" Lucy asked her.

Martin, whose social skills under ordinary circumstances were nearly nonexistent, was momentarily too stupefied by his apparent good fortune to speak. He stood behind Talia, who was siting next to Lucy at the bar, with his mouth agape and his eyes brimming with anticipation, like a starving dog eyeing a juicy chunk of prime rib.

"I'm from Beverly Hills," Talia purred, her English lightly inflected with a charmingly sultry accent. Sitting a safe two stools away, I found her voice, her gestures, her facial expressions to be intensely appetizing. I could only imagine what effect she was having on my nephew who had to be drowning in a sea of testosterone.

Talia, it later turned out, was from Tijuana and not Beverly Hills. Apparently, she *had* lived in Los Angeles for a number of years, but several realities east of Rodeo Drive.

When the conversation flagged almost at once, Lucy discreetly elbowed my nephew in the ribs and ordered him sotto voce to buy Talia a drink.

"Can I buy you a drink?" Martin asked her.

"Of course," Talia said. "I'll have a Corvoisier."

I winced at the realization that Talia was no cheap date, and the certain knowledge that ultimately the bar bill was going to land in my lap.

Halfway through her drink, Talia wondered aloud if there was a cigarette floating about nearby. My nephew, too busy gulping down excess saliva, failed to respond and Lucy was forced once again to nudge him forcefully in the ribs.

"Give her a cigarette!" she hissed into his ear.

By half past one the five of us were all blissfully smashed. A great deal of giggling was going on, as well as teasing and the tossing to and fro of innuendoes, the majority of which sailed right over my nephew's flatish head. Then, suddenly, Talia stood up and began to writhe in place.

"Let's dance," she said, favoring Martin with a lascivious look so hot it could have melted half the glassware on the bar.

To my utter shock, he replied, "I don't dance."

"Please!" she pleaded, her lips all in a pout.

"I don't dance," Martin said again.

"I dance," I said, trying to be helpful.

I'm not certain if, above the din of the ear-splitting music, Talia heard my offer. But Lucy did. Pressing both of her thumbs against my Adam's apple, my wife growled into my ear, "You left the house tonight a tenor. How would you like to go home a soprano?"

I'm not entirely clear as to how Martin and Talia's relationship progressed to the next level. My attention had become unaccountably diverted by two young Canadian women wearing micro skirts who were dancing with a great deal of enthusiasm inside one of the cages. I knew they were Canadians because they were wearing small maple leaf pins on their spandex tank tops right about where you would expect to find a left nipple. This, I was certain, must be some type of code. But what did it mean? Did they go both ways? Were they a tag team? Or were they simply advertising the fact that they were left-handed?

In any case, it was a code I was destined never to crack, because I was abruptly brought back to reality by my wife who suddenly spun me around to face the bar.

"Can you believe it?" she shouted into my ear.

Actually, I couldn't. Martin was sitting on a stool now and Talia was wrapped around him like an anaconda around a storm-bent tree. Tongues were leaping all over the place like flying squirrels high on speed. And Talia's Grade AAA backside was sliding around with such fluidity on my nephew's lap it gave every appearance of being lined with ball bearings.

"Jesus Christ!" I said to my wife.

"Am I good, or what?" Lucy said proudly. She meant as a matchmaker.

"Honey," I said with awe, "you're a magician."

Not for the first time I wondered what my life would have been like if Lucy had been my older sister instead of my wife.

The frenetic making out continued for another fifteen minutes, before Talia had to take a short break to go to the Ladies Room. Talia had now consumed five cognacs, and her gait as she teetered on her three-inch heels across the room was a mite unsteady. But the potential for a sprained ankle did not trouble me so much as did the bar bill, which was climbing steadily up into rarified regions I found most painful to contemplate. When I expressed my concern to

Lucy, she replied, "I wouldn't complain if I were you. It's still cheaper than hiring a hooker."

"Are you sure?"

Meanwhile Martin, moving like an over-wound wind-up toy, had jumped off of the stool and goose-stepped over to where we were standing. His eyes had the mad glare of a religious zealot and steam was pouring from his ears.

"Congratulations," I told him. "Here's five hundred pesos for the bar bill."

"Wait a minute," he said with sudden panic. "Are you leaving?"

"Yes," Lucy said. "We've done our part. The rest is up to you."

"But what do I do now?" Martin demanded.

"What do you mean?" Lucy said.

"I mean, I'm, you know, ready. To go all the way. With Talia."

"So what do you expect me to do," Lucy shouted in exasperation, "stick it in for you?"

My nephew's interminable visit was now drawing rapidly to a close, and I was beginning to feel guilty. Talia, the moment the free Corvosiers stopped flowing, had shamelessly dumped Martin with the promise that she would see him the next day. The next day he called her and they made a date, but of course she stood him up. Now he was moping around the house, more listless and morose than ever, and I felt that it was at least partly my fault. A really good uncle, I told myself, would not have refused to return to the scenes of horrific car accidents; nor would he have refused to enthusiastically aid and abet the massacre of innocent crustaceans.

"Look Martin," I said, placing my hands on his simian shoulders and looking deeply and earnestly into his rat-like eyes, "you're my only nephew. I'd like to see you have a good time. But I find myself at a loss. I mean, what would you really like to do? You know, tourist-wise. You name it, we'll do it."

Martin shrugged my hands off of his shoulders and knit his brow in concentration. Then, after a long pause he said, "I'd like to see the most gruesome, ghastly ghoulish tourist attraction in Mexico."

"Done," I said. "Be ready to leave at first light."

The eight-hour drive to Guanajuato was terribly uneventful: No roadside wrecks, no crippled canines, not even a plastered possum to break the tedium. Naturally, Martin was bored and restless. But not for long. He was about to have the touristic experience of a lifetime.

The small colonial city of Guanajuato has been called, and justly so, the most picturesque place in all of Mexico. Nestled amid steep green hillsides and running the length of a long narrow valley, it is liberally seasoned with architectural gems, steeped in culture and marinated in historical significance.

Nonetheless, its most popular tourist attraction (by a factor of five) is a collection of partially preserved human corpses which are referred to only half-euphemistically as "mummies".

When first informed many years earlier that there was a mummy museum in Guanajuato, I pictured something along Egyptian lines: vague human shapes all wrapped-up in centuries old strips of musty linen with stone sarcophagi, golden masks and all the other accessories one normally associates with such artifacts. Almost nothing could have been further from the truth.

While to some people, Egyptian mummies might seem a little creepy, Guanajuato mummies are downright revolting—which is to say, perfect for my nephew.

After paying our modest entrance fee, we were admitted to a long narrow building, the walls of which were lined with a series of glass cases. Inside these cases were a whole array of mummies wearing the remnants of the actual clothes they had been buried in. With the aid of wire, they had all been placed in a variety of casual upright poses.

There were men mummies, women mummies, children mummies, and even a baby bearing the sign, "World's Smallest Mummy".

"Though I've never been there," I told my nephew, "this is what I always imagined a bus stop in Miami Beach would look like."

"Wow!" Martin exclaimed. "Wow! Wow!"

"Yes, it is impressive," I agreed.

"But...but are they *real*?" My nephew could not believe his own eyes. "I mean," he added in a hoarse voice, "this isn't some kind of Disney-thing, is it?"

"No, they don't have Disney-things in Mexico."

"Then...they're real!" he gasped.

"Yes."

"But, but..."

Up until the moment we had set foot in the museum, so as to achieve the maximum impact, I had not even hinted at what we were about to see. Now I was duty-bound to give Martin some type of explanation, though I would have much preferred to give him a Valium instead.

"Apparently," I informed my bug-eyed nephew, "the soil of this region is exceedingly rich in certain minerals which act as natural preservatives."

"Preservatives?"

"Yes, you know, like they put in all that white bread you're always eating. Anyway, many years ago—no one seems to know exactly when—they had to move the local graveyard. And when they dug up the graves, instead of finding skeletons, they discovered all of these mummies."

"How come all their mouths are open?" Martin asked excitedly.

"Because they were all buried alive," I said with a straight face.

"Cool!"

"Just kidding, Martin. Actually it's a natural post-mortem skeletal-muscular phenomenon. Anyway, after they'd dug up a number of these folks, someone came up with the truly brilliant idea of putting them in cases and charging admission."

"Totally awesome," my nephew intoned.

Fifteen minutes is about the most a relatively normal person can stand to be inside the Guanajuato Mummy Museum. Naturally, my nephew set a new record. For almost two hours he stalked up and down that grisly chamber of horrors, visually absorbing every tooth, every strip of ligament, tendon, cartilage and parched skin in the entire repulsive place.

Finally, as the museum was closing for the day, he turned to me and said, "Uncle Gil, thanks. This is the best vacation I ever had!"

You're Better Off Walking

It was all my wife's fault, naturally. We were driving down Avenida Mexico, having just crossed the Bridge of Shrimps, when she said to me, "Imelda wants to open a taco stand."

"How nice," I said.

Imelda, one of my wife's oldest friends, was a manicurist with four unruly children, no husband, a boyfriend who was probably gay and a long sad history of financial problems which had driven her to our door again and again asking for loans, none of which she had ever repaid.

"She needs to borrow five thousand pesos," my wife explained. "Just to get her…"

"Forget it," I said. "Absolutely not."

"You…"

"Out of the question."

"You…"

"No!"

"You just ran a red light," my wife informed me.

"Oh."

Getting yourself pulled over by the police in Puerto Vallarta is not easy, especially if you happen to be a foreigner. In fourteen years of erratic, aggressive and often obnoxious driving (my instructor had been a former bus driver), I had only been pulled over twice.

I handed the absurdly friendly policeman my expired California driver's license, hoping that he would fail to notice the early Neolithic expiration date printed in bold letters on the bottom.

"This license is expired," the policeman said with a smile.

"Well, it may appear to be expired," I said, with the loving reluctance of a father who must finally explain to his son that there is no Santa Claus. "And it would actually, in fact, be expired," I went on, "had the State of California not recently passed the *Good Driver in Perpetuity* amendment to the motor vehicle code. Now, those drivers, like myself, who have a blemish free record, are spared the awful inconvenience of having to renew their licenses until they have reached the age of mandatory retirement."

Five minutes later the friendly policeman handed me a summons and told me that I could recover my rear license plate in City Hall, as soon as I paid the fine.

This incident, although innocuous in and of itself, left me shaken. Perhaps my wife was right: driving all over Mexico every year with a badly expired California license was probably prodding my luck. The police in Vallarta were nice enough, but what if we were to be stopped, for example, in Mexico City—the modern day equivalent of having your horse pulled over on the Siberian Steppes by Atilla the Hun.

I came to a momentous decision.

"Nacho," I told my best friend and expert on all things Mexican, "after fourteen years of living in your wonderfully convoluted country, I have finally decided to take the plunge."

Nacho sipped his third espresso of the day, and eyed me with alarm.

"Yes," I replied to his unspoken query, "I am going to attempt to acquire a Mexican driver's license."

Nacho shook his head slowly in disbelief.

"So tell me," I asked, "is it as much of an ordeal as they say?"

"Not too bad," Nacho said judiciously, "about like learning Portuguese."

"Oh, come on," I moaned.

"I don't know," Nacho said with concern, "you gringos lead such sheltered lives."

"So what are you saying, Nacho?"

"What I am saying, my friend, is you're better off walking."

My first stop was the office of the Secretary of Transport (ST). This was a less than inspiring edifice which I will describe in more detail later. Inside, on one of the walls were four large posters with faded lists of requirements printed by hand with a nearly dry magic marker. One poster was for women, one for men, one for minors and one for foreigners. I took out my pen and scrupulously copied down the extensive list for foreigners.

Uncertain what to do next, I decided to ask a uniformed woman what my first step should be. She smiled warmly and explained that first I had to purchase the official form. When I began to reach for my wallet, she said, "No, not here. You buy the form at the state tax office."

"Naturally," I said, "it wouldn't make much sense to buy it here."

"Of course not," she agreed.

The state tax office was located all the way across town, but acquiring my official form proved to be relatively easy: forty minutes in one line, and only thirty minutes in another.

Form in hand and only one hundred and fifty pesos poorer, I headed for my next stop, the optometrist. Though I had been told that any old optometrist would do, I opted for the one conveniently located just around the corner from the ST office.

Dressed in a brilliant white smock,the vision meister was totally bald and wore upon his enormous nose glasses so thick they looked like the bottoms of soda bottles. Squinting in the general direction of my navel, he said that my eyes looked fine to him and offered me a seat. The actual examination was pleasant, painless and lasted almost twenty seconds. When it was over I handed the doctor fifty pesos and he handed me a letter stating that my vision was excellent, top-notch, absolutely 20/20. We shook hands warmly and I left with the feeling that Ray Charles would have passed the exam as easily as I had.

Next it was off to my favorite instant photo ID shop, which had been in continuous operation for thirty years but still had no air conditioner. After making me wait in the broiling heat for twenty minutes while he and his compadre finished their dissection of the national soccer team's most recent dismal performance, the photographer handed me a towel.

"Have a towel," he said. "If you don't wipe off your face it'll come out all shiny in the photographs."

Like a dutiful son I mopped my dripping face with the towel, which looked clean but smelled like Mark McGwire's socks. An astonishingly short time later, I was rewarded with four tiny photos of a dry-faced man who looked like a cross between myself and an axe murderer.

Photos, good-vision certificate and official form in hand, I headed next for my landlady's house in order to acquire my "proof of address".

Since the water, electricity and phone bills were all in Señora Esperanza's name, every time I had to prove to a government agency that I lived where I said I did, Señora Esperanza was obliged to provide me with a letter stating that I lived in her house and attach to it several photocopies of my electric bill and her voter ID card.

Naturally Señora Esperanza had no typewriter, so she had to send her over-weight niece (who never met a burrito she didn't like) out in search of a professional typing service. The girl was gone for almost two hours, but I didn't mind as the delay allowed me to sample a plateful of my landlady's exquisite home-made tamales, and to loan the dear lady five-hundred pesos for a root canal on a badly infected molar which, with the help of the Virgin of Guadalupe, her dentist would hopefully be able to save.

When Señora Esperanza finally handed me the thick wad of documents, I asked her if she had a driver's license.

"No, why?" she asked without curiosity.

I explained to her that I needed to get my hands on two photocopies of the local driver's license of someone I supposedly knew—it was on the list of requirements for foreigners.

My landlady digested this for a moment and then told me that she had a nephew who might have a driver's license.

"But he's an irresponsible bum," she added. "So it's probably expired."

"What does he do for a living?" I asked.

"He's a bus driver," she said.

I thanked Señora Esperanza profusely for all her help, said good-bye and jogged around the corner to a taxi stand.

"I'll give you twenty pesos if you let me photocopy your driver's license," I told the first taxi-driver I could find.

"Sure, why not?" the man said, taking me, and who could blame him, for a deranged moron.

While I was at it I also made two copies of my passport and immigration papers. Now, as far as I could tell, I had all the documentation necessary (enough to stuff a small mattress), so I checked my watch (it was almost two) and headed back to the ST office.

Naturally, it was closed for the day.

The next morning I made my official appearance bright and early. I now had in my possession the following: one passport, several small yet exceedingly unflattering photographs of my head, an immigration book, copies of a taxi-driver's license, a good-vision certificate, an official form, numerous pieces of paper which taken collectively seemed to provide proof of my current address, and several copies of everything but my most recent stool analysis.

While most of Puerto Vallarta had over the years been modernized, updated, computerized and generally dragged kicking and screaming into something resembling the late twentieth century, the ST office had somehow been passed over.

It was a strange, sparsely furnished L-shaped room with twenty foot high ceilings from which dangled an impressive collection of cobwebs. The walls and floor were mostly bare and largely neglected. What appeared to be the official records were stored in a number of old and battered cardboard boxes scattered about the cement floor. And there was not a computer in sight, though I did count three manual typewriters.

The office furnishings consisted entirely of a quartet of scarred and dented metal desks placed strategically about the room. A short line of people was standing in front of one of these WW II vintage pieces, and I proceeded to join them.

An hour and a half later, it was my turn. A very friendly man inspected my bundle of documents and informed me that I had neglected to photocopy the official form, not to mention the good-vision certificate. A greener gringo than I might then have stopped to inquire where the nearest copy machine was located. But from long experience I knew that there is *always* such a device located within easy walking distance of all government offices. And so, in no time at all I was once again standing in line, four photocopies richer.

After twenty minutes I was able to get someone's attention again. He examined all of my papers with excruciating thoroughness, pronounced them to be in order and sent me to another desk to be finger-printed.

The finger-printer, once he had finished man-handling my thumb, directed me back to the first desk where I was informed that I would now have to take the legendary written exam—at a third desk. At the third desk I was politely asked to take a seat.

Thirty minutes later a uniformed woman handed me a pencil and five well-used sheets of paper on which were printed forty-nine barely legible multiple-choice questions.

The written exam was a joint creation of Franz Kafka and the Marquis de Sade. Neither common sense nor knowledge of local transit law was of any value in attempting to unravel the surreal and labyrinthine logic which lay beneath the questions. I might as well have been taking the Bar Exam in Pakistani. A typical example:

Q. What is advisable to check before undertaking a long trip?

    a: tires, registration and seat-belt
    b: brakes, first-aid kit and spare-tire
    c: lights, oil level and maps
    d: none of the above

By the time I had circled the letter "C" on question forty-nine (just for the hell of it), I was feeling physically ill. I handed the completed test to a dapper looking fellow who had taken the uniformed woman's place at desk number three. Judging by his imperious demeanor, he appeared to be the highest-ranking official in the office. With an air of supreme self-importance he proceeded to check my score. When he had finished, he simply sat there contemplating his freshly manicured fingernails, an annoyed expression besmirching his bloated face.

I had seen this look on the faces of government officials before, and it did not bode well.

Finally, I could stand it no longer and asked, "How did I do?"

"Not good," he said somberly.

When he failed to offer any additional information, I asked, "Well, how many did I get wrong?"

"Twenty-three," he replied menacingly.

I now asked what, to someone who has not spent a great deal of time in Mexico, might appear to be a stupid question. "So, does that mean I passed?"

The man shook his head gravely, got up and disappeared into what I assumed was the bathroom.

When, a good while later, he returned to his desk, he sat down and began to stare at his nails again.

"Well?" I said finally.

"Well, you failed the test," he said.

"You know," I told him, "if I took that test every day for the rest of my life, I still wouldn't pass it."

"Yes," he agreed.

"I've been driving for over thirty years," I said. "I know how to drive. What I don't know is how to pass that damn test."

"Yes," he said with sudden compassion, "I understand. And I want to help you."

At this heartfelt expression of an official's selfless urge to help extricate a troubled foreigner from his desperate dilemma, I heaved a healthy sigh of relief.

Then from my breast pocket I extracted a colored rectangular piece of paper which had been folded again and again until it formed a compact little square.

"Thank you so much for helping me," I told my new friend as we executed an awkward handshake.

"It is my pleasure," he said graciously.

Five minutes later I was handed my new driver's license, valid, thank God, well into the next century—it would take me at least that long to save up enough money to pay for its renewal.

Lucy and
the Mushroom Witch

My wife, God bless her, is always equal to any challenge. And so when I informed her of our decision to make the tortuous twenty hour drive up into the heart of the remote Mazateco Mountains in search of Doña Marta, the last surviving mushroom witch, her reply was: "Are we sure we want to do this?"

"Yes," I said.

"Then I'm with you, baby. As long as you realize one thing."

"Which is?"

"You're out of your goddamn mind," she said, kissing me tenderly on the cheek.

The turnoff for Huautla was clearly marked. Unfortunately, it was clearly marked with the name of a different town. But this being Mexico, we ignored the misinformation and headed up the steep, winding road, penetrating higher and deeper (if that is possible) into the obscenely lush and exotically beautiful "land of the little people".

The road to Huautla was paved, after a fashion. It was also decorated with a dazzling variety of potholes, crisscrossed by impromptu creeks and littered with innumerable minor landslides. Despite the spectacular scenery (thousand foot cliffs, roaring waterfalls and ferns the size of small cottages), this, the last leg of our trip, proved to be something of an ordeal.

"Do you think we're going to die on this road?" Lucy asked as our VW bug fishtailed wildly around a particularly frightening curve.

"Probably," I grunted, my knuckles white on the steering wheel.

"That's nice," Lucy said with spectacular calm.

A short while later when our vehicle began to slide *backwards* on a frighteningly steep and muddy grade, Lucy announced, "I think we're falling behind schedule."

"We're not falling anywhere yet," I said, downshifting into first gear and praying with great single-mindedness to the Virgin of Guadalupe.

After slipping to within fifteen feet of the edge of a bona-fide abyss, our smoking tires finally managed to obtain a tenuous grip on the muddy surface, and we began to inch forward again.

Several hours of this slow torture later, after passing through one layer of cloud and then another, we finally arrived at the small town of Huautla de Jiminez in the southern state of Oaxaca.

Huautla was the kind of place which should have remained forever lost in time and space. It was not near anything, except perhaps God. It had no industry, miserable weather and was populated almost entirely by Indians who barely spoke the language of their own country.

But a little old lady named Maria Sabina would by the late 1960's attract to Huautla, like muddy iron filings to a magnet, thousands of Mexican and American hippies, as well as the Beatles, Mick Jagger, Bob Dylan and even the President of Mexico, who declared Maria to be a "National Icon", and who personally promised to give to the impoverished mushroom witch a substantial sum of money, which of course she never received.

Huautla had one main street which ran along the side of a mountain. Both the uphill and downhill sides of this street were plagued by frequent mudslides. The only place in town to eat an actual meal was a small wobbly shack built on stilts overhanging a cliff. We ate at this establishment, which specialized in unrecognizable chicken parts, every day for two weeks, but never once lingered over our coffee.

In Huautla you could never be certain exactly where you were at. The whole area was beset by swirling mists and low-flying clouds, so that everything was continually disappearing and then reappearing again. The people spoke in bird-like whispers, were intensely shy and so tiny that from a distance they all looked like children. As my wife and I lumbered down the muddy streets in our high-heeled miner's boots and full-length orange ponchos, couples huddled in doorways stared at us and whispered to each other in awe-filled tones: "Grande!"

Since our arrival took place just as it was about to get dark, we set about at once to find a hotel room. We soon discovered that there were three hotels in town: The Bad, The Ugly and The Uglier. Lucy, always thorough to a fault, insisted that we inspect all three establishments before making a decision.

The first hotel, which was small and completely unoccupied, had tiny, dark damp rooms with no windows and doors which only partially closed. But its worst feature by far was an awful penetrating odor.

"Did someone die in this room recently?" I asked the young man in charge.

"No," he replied with the utmost seriousness, "no one has stayed in this room for months."

The second hotel, also empty, was even smaller than the first and lacked, among other things, any semblance of indoor plumbing.

"Where do you go to the bathroom?" I asked the manager. The man, whose Spanish was almost non-existent, shrugged and pointed with his chin in the direction of the back yard.

But the third hotel (our last hope, short of getting arrested) was a wonderful surprise. Twice the size of its two competitors, it consisted of almost twelve rooms. These rooms, though small, damp and dingy, did contain windows, indoor plumbing and lockable doors. The owners, two very short brothers with polio, proudly informed us that they provided fresh towels (damp and the size of dinner napkins) on a daily basis, as well as unlimited hot water for forty-five minutes almost every morning—between the hours of six and seven.

These brothers, whose names were Mario and Julio, were in their early thirties and difficult to tell apart. In fact they might have been twins. Even with the aid of crutches they were barely able to get around. Consequently they spent most of their time in a small room behind the reception area watching TV with their friends, drinking beer and sleeping.

The reception area, just a bend in the damp gloomy second floor hallway, was identifiable as such by its small high counter. Julio leaned against this counter eyeing me curiously. Lucy and I had already inspected a room and decided that this hotel was undoubtedly our best option.

"So which rooms are available, Mario?" I asked.

"My name is Julio," he corrected me. "All of them," he added.

"I see," I said. "And what's the going rate?"

"For two people?" he asked. His Spanish was basic, but easy to understand.

"Yes," I said after a pause, as if I'd had to think it over.

"Ten pesos," he said, which at that precise moment came to a little over three dollars.

"And does that include the soap and toilet paper?" I asked, hoping to extract, with my feeble attempt at humor, a smile from his somber face.

"No," Julio replied.

I paid Julio for two days in advance and he gave me a nondescript sort of key. The key had no number on it, so I felt compelled to ask, "Which room?"

"Whichever you want. The key opens all the doors and you're the only guests."

After much traipsing in and out, Lucy and I decided on number eleven. It had a nice clean concrete floor, tastefully mildewed cinder block walls, a reassuringly solid cast iron twin bed, an unpainted wood chair with three legs and a killer view of the wall of fog which lay almost perpetually outside the only window—conveniently located inside the shower stall.

"Look at this," I told my wife as she joined me at the window. "I'll bet on a clear day you can see all the way across the street." As it was, the only visible object at the moment was a utility pole located about a meter from our noses.

The air of unreality, which hung about Huautla along with the clouds, became more pronounced as our stay progressed.

"Did you ever have one of those dreams," I asked Lucy that night, "where you get off at the wrong bus stop and suddenly find yourself in the *Twilight Zone*?"

"No, I don't think so," she replied.

At breakfast the next day, after we had ordered scrambled eggs and lukewarm beans (the other choice was scrambled eggs and lukewarm rice), the ten-year-old waitress asked us if we wanted bread as well.

"Yes," I said. "That would be nice."

"You can't have any," she said.

"Why not?" Lucy asked.

"All the bakeries are closed," she said.

"Oh, why is that?" I asked.

The young girl's eyes went wide with wonder. "Only God knows," she replied.

After breakfast we went for a walk in a light drizzle up and down the main street. Visibility was almost forty feet, so there was quite a bit to see.

"Nice hardware store," I said.

"Yes, their selection of chicken wire appears to be outstanding," Lucy said.

"I wonder what used to be there?" I said, pointing to a large gaping wound on the downhill side of the street, in the midst of which concrete footings lay forlornly on their sides like so many unconscious drunks.

"The Opera House?" Lucy opined.

At that moment the curtain of fog lifted entirely and we saw for the first time that we were surrounded by steep, lush green mountains. I had time to count four separate waterfalls before the fog descended once again causing our marvelous view to vanish as suddenly as it had appeared.

After lunch, a plate of deep fried chicken shins with rice *and* beans, I told Lucy that it was time to find Doña Marta, the last surviving mushroom witch. Having said that, I quickly realized that I had no idea how to proceed.

Due to the ambiguous nature of the Mexican criminal justice system, we had no way of knowing with certainty what was legally acceptable and what was not. On the one hand, it might be perfectly all right to buy magic mushrooms from, say, the chief of police. On the other hand, merely asking after the whereabouts of Doña Marta could turn out to be a serious felony. And despite Huautla's small size, it was simply brimming with keepers of the peace, who despite *their* small size were no doubt perfectly capable of incarcerating erring gringos should the need arise.

Since it was by far the largest town in the entire area, Huautla acted as the regional headquarters for many government agencies, among them the military, the state police, the federal police, the municipal police and so on and so forth. Our unusual status (we were, at the moment, the only foreigners in town, not to mention the only human beings over five feet four inches tall) made the task of keeping a low profile while searching for the mushroom witch problematical to say the least.

"What I think we need to do," I told my wife, "is look for someone *hip*."

"*Hip*?" Lucy said. "*Here*?"

"Well, I admit the pickings may be slim, but I'm sure we can find at least one person who we can trust not to turn us in to the police."

And so, we spent the next two days skulking about the town of Huautla de Jiminez, attempting to stay dry and hinting in the most vague fashion possible to the occasional likely prospect that we wouldn't be adverse to receiving information as to the whereabouts of someone who might have some specialized knowledge relating to edible fungi.

So fearful were we of being more specific that apparently no one we spoke to had even the slightest idea what we were talking about. One longhaired Indian, who must have assumed that we were lost, attempted to give us directions to the nearest beach, which was over three hundred miles away.

On our third evening in town, Lucy and I were walking up and down the dark, mist-shrouded street looking for a place to buy some apples when we came upon a small fruit stand which loomed up out of the wet inky night like a mirage. The proprietress, a tiny crone all dressed in black, stood in the shadows, her face completely obscured by the dark shawl which covered her head. In a high, creaking voice she asked if she could help us.

"We'd like some apples," Lucy said.

"I have apples," the crone croaked.

"Give me two kilos, please," Lucy said.

When the transaction was almost completed, the old woman asked casually, "Have you had your *hongos* yet?"

Suddenly, our hearts began to race. Was this a trap? Was this tiny, hunched-over fruit vendor actually a police informant? Or was this the lucky chance we'd been waiting for?

"Hongos?" I said innocently. "Are they very good to eat?"

"They don't taste that good," the crone said, "but they put you on a hell of a trip."

"Oh, *those* hongos," I said.

"Yes, *those* hongos." It was apparent from the crone's tone of voice that I wasn't fooling her for a minute.

"Well, you know," I said, "we tried those when we were younger, but we're too old for that kind of thing now."

"You should really have some hongos," the old fruit vendor insisted. "Everybody comes here for the hongos."

"Oh, is that right," I said. "Aren't they illegal?"

"Illegal!" the crone snorted. "Hurumph! In this country, it's only illegal if you get caught."

"Yes, well…"

"You should go and see Doña Marta in San Carlos," the old lady persisted. "She can get you some really good hongos."

"Maybe another time," I said. "Buenas noches."

San Carlos, only an hour away, was the largest of the tiny towns which surrounded Huautla on all sides. It would be a piece of cake, I believed, to locate Doña Marta there. But so great was our fear of being arrested that still we could not make up our minds.

The Mazateco Indians are famous for their beautiful embroidery. The next day we decided to do some shopping. We entered, in the course of the morning, five or six small stalls filled with embroidered rebozos, dresses and blouses. In every stall, the tiny salesperson asked us the same question: "Have you had your hongos yet?"

It was as if a veil had suddenly been lifted and the whole town had collectively decided that we absolutely must have our magic mushrooms.

Then we began to discover T-shirts and post cards for sale with magic mushrooms emblazoned boldly all over them. Where they had been for the previous several days is a mystery I have yet to solve.

Back at the hotel, Julio (or was it Mario) asked us if we'd had our mushrooms yet! When we replied in the negative, he acted annoyed. From under the counter he took out a stack of postcards, all depicting different types and sizes of magic mushrooms.

"This one," he said, "is the *pajarito*. It is the prettiest."

The *pajarito* looked to me more like a deformed umbrella than a small bird, and it was about as pretty as a bunion, but all I said was, "Very nice."

"And this one," he said, passing me another card, "is called the *San Isidro*. It is the largest."

"Is San Isidro the patron saint of mushrooms?" I asked, just to say something.

"Not that I know of," Julio or Mario replied. "And this one," he went on, indicating a small dark mushroom which looked exactly like a pygmy's penis, "is called the *derumbe* (landslide). It is the most powerful of them all. If I were you, I would be careful with this one."

"I have no intention of eating any of these mushrooms," I lied, having already decided that it would be a *derumbe* or nothing.

"Of course," he said.

At dinner that evening, the taciturn waitress who rarely opened her mouth, even to breathe, asked us if we'd had our mushrooms yet. When we replied in the negative, she said testily, "Why not?"

"That does it," I told my wife. "Everybody thinks we're a pair of idiots because we haven't had our mushrooms yet. Tomorrow we go to San Carlos."

Doña Marta, the diminutive mushroom witch, had long, straight, gray streaked hair, lively eyes and an enigmatic smile. We had been told by friends in Mexico City that she was a "white" witch. We had also been told, by friends in Guadalajara, that she was a "black" witch. Naturally we had assumed that she was neither. Then the engine compartment of our utterly reliable Volkswagen bug burst inexplicably into flame as we were cruising the small town of San Carlos looking for her house.

Several minutes and much hysterical activity later, as we stood staring forlornly at the still smoldering cables, an old Mazateco Indian hobbled over to see what we were up to. My wife asked him if he happened to know where Doña Marta's house was.

"You're standing right in front of it," he said.

The mushroom witch was cautiously cordial as she served us coffee in the dirt-floored living room of her modest adobe home. She had to know why we were there, but for one esoteric motive or another she had decided that before more serious subjects could be broached we must first engage in an hour-long session of small talk.

That is, it began as small talk, but quickly metamorphosed into a full-blown interrogation. Smiling pleasantly, Doña Marta proceeded to grill us relentlessly about every aspect of our lives, from the cradle to the present moment.

On several occasions I attempted to introduce the topic of hongos into the conversation. The first time she ignored me completely. The second time she whispered conspiratorially, "Not now, there are too many people around."

There was in fact, as near as I could tell, nobody around at all.

As we slogged through the second half-hour of chitchat my perception of the mushroom witch kept shifting in and out of focus. Was she being shrewd? Was all this small talk just a device designed to drive the price up? Was she paranoid? Was she afraid that we were government anti-narcotics agents trained to speak Spanish with impeccable gringo accents? Or was she testing us the way a shaman tests a potential disciple? I decided to embrace the last hypothesis, as it coincided nicely with my romantic image of a Mexican bruja.

"So you live in Puerto Vallarta?" Doña Marta asked for the second time.

"Yes," Lucy replied.

"And that's why your Spanish is so good," she said doubtfully.

"Our Spanish is really only so-so," I said modestly.

"No, no, it is excellent," Doña Marta said. "I have met many foreigners but very few have spoken Spanish so well," she added, a faint note of suspicion tainting her mellifluous voice. "And you used to be a hairdresser, Lucy?" she asked my wife, also for the second time.

"Yes," Lucy replied patiently.

"Then I suppose you know how to give a permanent?" Doña Marta asked.

"Well, I haven't done one for twenty years, but it's, you know, like riding a bicycle—something you never forget."

"I see," Doña Marta said, staring mystically off into space. "I never had a bicycle. Please excuse me."

As she rose from her chair and glided gracefully from the room, I was certain that our horse was about to come in, that she was going to return in a few minutes with an armload of hongos, magic potions and possibly even an ancient tome full of secret incantations penned by the Dhali Llama himself.

When she returned ten minutes later, her arms were indeed laden with small round objects, her hands did truly grasp an ancient looking vial of dark liquid, as well as an equally ancient little book.

"Oh shit," Lucy said in English, shocking me nearly senseless, since my wife never cursed in any language.

"The solution is very, very old, but I believe it will still work," Doña Marta said.

Everything went in and out of focus for a moment, as if I'd been hexed. Then the mushrooms turned into small hair rollers, the vial of magic bug juice into permanent solution and the ancient text into a set of instructions—not by the Dahli Llama, but by Lady Clairol.

"Is this going to take long?" I asked Lucy in English.

"The rollers are tiny. Her hair is down to her butt and if the solution is really that old...I'm figuring at least five hours," Lucy concluded unhappily.

As the long tortuous process began I decided to excuse myself and go look for a mechanic.

The wee town of San Carlos was, I soon discovered, home to only one mechanic. I found him in the town square working inside the engine compartment of a five-ton truck. The mechanic, like most Mazateco Indians, was truly tiny and instead of leaning over the engine compartment, he had curled himself up inside of it. His entire upper torso was, in fact, completely entwined in cables, springs and wires, reminding me of Gregory Peck in the last scene of *Moby*

Dick. He told me that he was too busy to work on my car and that I should come back later.

"When?" I asked.

"Two or three days," he replied.

"Did you say days or hours?" I asked the mechanic, hoping that I had misunderstood his garbled Spanish.

"I said days," he replied, "but it might be a week."

Walking forlornly back to Doña Marta's house, I ran into her son, Constantino. After explaining my predicament to him, he offered to try to fix the car himself.

"Are you a mechanic?" I asked hopefully.

"No, not really," he replied.

I left Constantino, a pre-Hispanic kitchen knife in one hand and a partially liquefied roll of black electrical tape in the other, sitting cross-legged in the dirt and squinting uncertainly into the bowels of the charred engine compartment. Then, slogging through three inches of mud and past a pack of ravenous pigs, I made my way into the courtyard to check on Lucy and the mushroom witch.

My wife is the kind of person who can find delight in the most unlikely situations. I found her and Dona Marta chatting merrily away, giggling and carrying on like a couple of schoolgirls. If this was a test, Lucy was passing it with preternaturally flying colors.

When Doña Marta took a trip to the bathroom, I asked Lucy how it was going.

"Slow," she replied. "I've never seen hair so straight in my life."

"It's probably part of the test," I said.

"What test?"

"Never mind," I said, "What about the mushrooms? Anything about the mushrooms?"

"No. Every time I mention something she says to wait until later, that there's too many people around."

"Have you seen any people?"

"No."

Suddenly, I had an inspiration.

"Maybe she means dead people," I said. "You know, spirits. Maybe there are unfavorable spirits floating around here."

"Unfavorable spirits?" Lucy said. "You been getting too much sun today, or what?"

"Well...never mind."

According to Lucy's calculations I had about another four hours to kill, so I decided to reconnoiter the area, after first checking with Constantino.

Constantino had been joined by his cousin Marcos, who was visiting from Zacatecas and who had been drinking cane alcohol continuously for about fifteen years. Constantino was still sitting on the ground meditating on the engine compartment. The mushroom witch's son was, as far as I could tell, perfectly sober. Marcos, on the other hand...

"Mucho gusto!" Marcos exclaimed with enthusiasm, shaking my hand, which he then refused to release.

"Delighted to meet you, Marcos," I said. "Could you please let go of my hand?"

"Mucho gusto!" Marcos repeated, as he continued to grip my hand.

Finally, after much tugging back and forth, I put my whole weight into it and managed to wrench my hand free, causing Marcos to topple sideways onto the dusty ground. He made an elaborate show of dusting himself off, readjusting his shirt and fixing his hair. Then he looked up at me, held out his hand and yelled, "MUCHO GUSTO!"

Rejecting Marcos' proffered extremity, I turned around and headed up into the hills, where I came across a gaping wound in the Earth, a doorway to one of the deepest and most extensive systems of caves and caverns in the world. And as I stood there staring down into its murky depths, a scene from the previous day began, for no apparent reason, to replay itself in my mind.

Lucy had finally come a bit unglued over the sad condition of our towels and asked if I could attempt to procure something better.

"Better how?" I asked.

"Better bigger. Better dryer. Better cleaner. Better…"

It had been raining, sprinkling or heavily misting non-stop since our arrival in Huautla and the hotel hallway was so damp stalactites had begun to form on the banister. Nonetheless, I went searching for one of the brothers to see if he could somehow magically produce a pair of dry towels.

I encountered Julio in the small room behind the reception counter, and asked him about the possibility of procuring a pair of fresher and dryer towels.

"No problem," he said. Less true words had never been spoken.

It took Julio an agony-filled five minutes just to get out of his chair and arrange his crutches. Up to my eyebrows in guilt, I said with feigned nonchalance, "Listen, Julio, why don't you just tell me where you keep the towels and I'll go get them myself."

"I'm Mario," he said, breathing heavily. "I'll have those towels for you in a minute."

I could never hope to adequately describe how incredibly awful I felt as I watched Mario make his unbelievably slow, tortured, crooked way down the long dark hall to the linen closet. But once I had set the poor fellow in motion, what could I do?

Thirty minutes later he finally returned, bathed in sweat, gasping for air and weaving perilously about on his antiquated metal crutches. The two towels, which were no larger or dryer than the ones we already had, were tucked under his left arm. All at once he made an odd lunging motion and I thought for sure that he was going to go over the railing and tumbling down to his doom two floors below. But he was merely attempting to grab the towels out from under his left arm with his right hand without losing his grip on the crutch, which was of course impossible.

"Can I help you with those towels?" I offered, unable to watch his painful contortions any longer.

"No, I've got them," Mario panted, determined to finish what he had started.

"Are you sure?" I asked him.

By way of reply he made two more tries for the towels, his entire body teetering dangerously with each attempt, like a tall stack of dishes. I knew that at any moment he was going to topple, and that I had to stop him. But standing between us like an impassable gate was the poor fellow's pride.

Either I am going to humiliate him by forcing my help upon him, I reasoned, or else he is going to kill himself over those two stupid towels. Deciding finally that his pride would heal itself faster than a broken neck, I reached out, grabbed the towels and yanked. The towels came free easily enough, but unfortunately, so did his right crutch. As my host began to go down, I grabbed him in a bear hug, which is how Lucy found us a few seconds later, embracing awkwardly there in the dingy hallway.

"Am I interrupting something?" she asked.

After Lucy had departed with her two fresh damp towels, I lingered there for a few minutes to chat with Mario hoping to dispel our mutual embarrassment. The potential range of our overlapping interests being somewhat limited, I decided to ask him about the satellite dishes.

Oddly enough for a town which had barely limped into the sixteenth century, Huautla was home to over fifty satellite dishes, all of which seemed to be malfunctioning at the same time. The dishes had been sold on the slow-payment plan to the innocent townspeople and were not adjustable. They were installed pointing more or less at a given satellite, and there they remained, their burden of debt passing from one generation of Mazatecans to the next.

"So how many channels do you get on your TV?" I asked Mario.

"About twelve," he replied.

At that time in Puerto Vallarta my friends with dishes were receiving over two hundred.

"Why so few?" I asked.

Mario shrugged with the utter fatalism so typical of poor Mexicans. I might as well have asked him why we all had to die.

"And why is the reception so bad?" I went on, desperate to get some kind of conversation going. "Where I live everyone with a satellite dish gets perfect reception."

Mario's reply was short and to the point. "You don't live here," he said.

After what must have been an hour I was finally able to tear my gaze away from that black hole in the Earth and return to Doña Marta's place. Constantino, standing with his arms folded against his chest and beaming with pride, had miraculously repaired the Volkswagen. I thanked him profusely, gave him fifty pesos and vigorously shook his hand, which made his cousin Marcos jealous because once again I had refused to shake his. Then I waded through the mud and past the pigs to see how my wife was making out.

Doña Marta was practically all rolled-up and Lucy was beginning to fade along with the daylight. My wife had been struggling with the bruja's hair now for almost seven hours.

Finally, the permanent process complete, the mushroom witch invited us to sit with her in the kitchen and have another cup of coffee.

"Well," she said, "now that we are finally alone we can talk about the hongos."

"That's wonderful, Doña Marta," I said happily.   "I guess what I'd like to know is, could you possibly sell us some?"

"Oh, I would never sell the magic hongos," she replied. "They are a gift from the Great Spirit."

"That's a really beautiful sentiment, Doña Marta," I said sincerely. "So then, in the spirit of the Great Spirit, do you think you could find some to give to us?"

"Of course," she said quickly, "if you wished to express your gratitude with a small symbolic gift…"

"Of course," I said at once. "What kind of a small symbolic gift would you consider appropriate?"

"Oh, I think a hundred and fifty pesos," Doña Marta said, "would be about right. But..."

"But what?"

"It will be my great pleasure to procure for you the magic mushrooms," Doña Marta said formally. "But the season for hongos is past, so you will have to come back next year."

"Next year?"

"Yes," the mushroom witch said sweetly. "And perhaps when you return you could bring me some of that wonderful gringo hair conditioner. I'm not getting any younger, you know, and neither is my hair."

Seven And
One Half Virgins

I was sitting in the stately shaded square in downtown Oaxaca perusing the Mexico City News when a man carrying a carved wooden pig lurched into the side of my iron bench.

"*Chinga su madre!*" he told the bench.

His name, I would soon discover, was Don Faustino Hidalgo Cardenas. He reminded me, with his battered felt hat and three-day beard, of Humphrey Bogart in the African Queen. I liked him at once; it never occurred to me that he might be a dangerous lunatic.

"Are you all right?" I asked, as he continued to curse the bench.

"Two hundred pesos," he replied in a rusty voice. "And not one centavo less!"

"What?"

"Hundred and eighty," he said, eyeing me with hostility. "I'm fifty years old and I'm not putting up with your shit a second longer. That's my last offer."

"Are you selling the pig?" I asked, hiding a smile.

"No, I'm selling my ass," he said. "And I'll tell you something else, you ignorant excuse for a fool: this is no ordinary pig."

"I can see that."

Protruding out from beneath the beast's wooden belly was a grotesquely over-sized set of wooden genitalia.

"It's a macho pig," Don Faustino said with pride. "I made it with these two hands."

The smashed sculptor began to spread his palms, seeming to forget for the moment that he was holding the carving.

"Watch out!" I yelled.

"Oh, so you like it," he said with a wily smile.

"Well...yes. In fact, I'll buy it."

The purchase of the pig, it soon became apparent, would be no routine transaction.

"There must be negotiations," Don Faustino declared.

"But why?" I protested. "The price has been set."

"Between *men*," he said, "things must be done properly. Important matters are still open for discussion."

"What matters?" I demanded. "Everything has been settled."

"Nothing has been settled, yet. Follow me."

Don Faustino led me to a nearby cantina, which at eleven thirty in the morning was nearly deserted, but redolent still with the stale fetid odors of nights past. In one corner of the small room was an enormous old jukebox. Weaving erratically, my new friend approached the archaic metal monster and shouted, "Musica!"

"You have to put money in it," the bartender said.

"I know that, you dimwitted worm," Don Faustino replied.

A moment later the entire cantina was vibrating with the voice of Vicente Fernandez (accompanied by a screeching off-key Don Faustino) belting out at maximum volume the Mexican male's macho anthem, *El Rey*:

"Whether I have money or not,
I always do what I want.
And my word is the lawwwww!
I don't have a throne or a queen,
And nobody understands me,
But I'm still the kinggggg!"

Halfway through the second stanza our negotiations began in earnest. Don Faustino's first demand was that I consume four shots of mescal one after the other. The quality of mescal served in those seedy Oaxaca cantinas was the lowest of the low. I would have been better off chugalugging lighter fluid.

"Sorry, Don Faustino," I said, " I never drink before noon."

"What?" he cried. "What are you trying to tell me? *Estoy tratando con un pinche puto*?" (Am I dealing with a lousy male whore?).

From previous experience I knew that I would have to put Don Faustino in his place at once.

"The last man who called me a puto," I said, struggling not to laugh as I leapt theatrically to my feet, "I ripped his heart out and fed it to my dog. Apologize now, you miserable bastard, or you're a dead man!"

"Ah, that's the ticket!" Don Faustino said, staggering off his stool and embracing me. "That's the way a *man* does it! That's how a son of *mine* would do it!"

With a little difficulty I managed to escape Don Faustino's sloppy but sturdy embrace. But my reprieve lasted only a moment. For the next hour I sat at my stool attempting vainly to conclude our transaction while the sculptor, splattering my face repeatedly with droplets of mescal-scented saliva, professed his undying affection for me over and over, making me swear on my mother's honor ("if she has any") that I would visit him at his ranchito the very next day.

Just to be rid of the drunken, slobbering pest, I promised that I would.

Six months later I did in fact contact Don Faustino by telephone; his heroically endowed wooden pig had created a minor sensation in my shop, and I wanted to put an order in for more.

The sculptor lived in one of those remote mountain villages where the entire population shares a single telephone, located as a rule in a small general store and manned by a sorority of rude, taciturn women.

"I would like to speak with Don Faustino Hidalgo Cardenas," I told the woman who answered my call on the eleventh ring.

"Who?"

"Don Faustino Hidalgo Cardenas."

"Who?"

"The sculptor."

"The what?"

"The man who carves wooden animals with huge... um..."

"Faustino?"

"Yes, yes, Faustino!"

"Call back in twenty minutes," she said, and hung up.

When I called back twenty minutes later, a different woman's voice told me: "Call back in twenty minutes."

After being told on five successive occasions to call back in twenty minutes, I was finally treated to the hoarse virile voice of Don Faustino himself, who sounded completely sober. To my even greater surprise, he remembered exactly who I was.

"The gringo from Puerto Vallarta," he cried into the mouthpiece. "Of course I remember you."

In accordance with Mexican custom, Don Faustino and I exchanged a long string of pointless pleasantries. Then I explained to him that I wished to place an order for twelve of his sculptures. Sober, Don Faustino was the soul of cooperation. Prices, models, sizes and dates were agreed upon with incredible ease. Finally, wishing each other good health and prosperity, we said good-bye.

Normally, my wife accompanies me every inch along the way of our annual buying trips throughout southern and central Mexico. But on this occasion, due to the extreme remoteness of Don Faustino's village and the vague reports we had heard of "disturbances" in the area, she agreed reluctantly that I should go alone. So that she would not feel completely abandoned, I left her with most of our cash, all of our credit cards and a Last Will and Testament I had hastily put together the night before.

My wife's departing words to me, said only half in jest, were: "Don't look at any other women."

I left Oaxaca City at first light, hoping to arrive by noon, pick up my sculptures, spend an hour or so schmoozing with my host, and then return to town before dark. That was my plan and it seemed like a good one. Unfortunately, what I had no way of knowing at the time was that Don Faustino had a demented plan of his own.

Due to the nonspecific disturbances (I subsequently learned that earlier in the week a new guerilla group calling itself the "EPR", which sounded like but was not related to the Environmental Protection Agency, had murdered several policemen in a neighboring town.), the authorities had installed a roadblock manned by the Federal Judicial Police just outside the City limits.

The particular officer with whom I had the unparalleled pleasure of conversing was curious as to who I was and where I was going—information I was delighted to supply. But words alone did not seem to satisfy him, so I handed the heavily armed policeman my business card.

Like an archaeologist scrutinizing some rare find, the Judicial studied my card with excruciating care. He even turned it over to examine the back, which of course was blank.

"This is your card?" he asked suspiciously.

I replied courteously that it was.

"You live in Puerto Vallarta?" he asked.

"Yes," I said, patiently informing him of this fact for the third time.

The Judicial took several steps away from my car and began to stare off into space. With nothing better to do, I held on to the top of the steering wheel and did the same.

Time passed.

More time passed.

The Judicial began to study my card again, for what reason I could not even begin to imagine, unless he was thinking of borrowing the design for one of his own:

Sargento Ruben Morales Mendoza
Especialista en:
Roadblocks, Bribes and Bar Mitzvahs

After what seemed like an awfully long time, just to test the waters, I decided to start the engine of my car. The Judicial continued to stare intently at my card. I put the vehicle into gear. More staring.

"Why don't you keep it," I told him. Then, holding my breath, I pulled slowly away. The Judicial stifled a yawn, but did not shoot me.

For an entire hour I drove without interruption. Then I pulled off the highway and onto a dirt road, which three separate taxi drivers had assured me was *not* a good road.

"*Es muy, muy malo,*" one had told me.

"*Es pesimo, ese camino!*" (That road is terrible) another had said.

"*Puta madre!*" (Whore-mother!) the third had exclaimed.

The road was in fact the worst upon which I had ever driven: a spine-jarring, kidney-rattling, jaw-breaking stretch of deeply rutted, dust-shrouded hell.

The village of Santa Maria de Los Cielos into which I crawled, battered and bruised, three hours later, could not have been less picturesque. Belying its lovely name, it was dry, dusty, desolate and heartbreakingly poor. Don Faustino had said that he would be waiting for me in the tiny square beside the over-sized church. Naturally, he wasn't there. But I had no trouble finding his house. A pair of dust-coated men, who looked like unemployed Hollywood banditos, explained to me that it was at the top of the hill, at the edge of a cliff—just keep going till you can't go anymore.

"How will I know if I've gone too far?" I asked. The brutal heat was already addling my brain.

"You'll know if you've gone too far," the one with more teeth told me, "because all your bones'll be broken".

"Or you'll be dead," the other added helpfully.

Trudging beneath the cruel midday sun up the narrow dusty track, I passed a dozen small miserable shacks, a handful of skinny goats, several disoriented roosters and four or five starving dogs. But no people.

Just as I had been told, the path ended without warning at the edge of a sheer cliff. On my left was an abyss. On my right, hugging the ridge, was a small compound containing three large well-maintained shacks, a small rustic corral and a fenced-in garden: in short, the Versailles of Santa Maria de Los Cielos.

The view from Don Faustino's property would have been spectacular had there only been something worth looking at. The limitless expanse of dry tormented hillsides, spotted with dead trees and the occasional scraggly cactus, did little to please the eye.

Checking my watch I noted with satisfaction that it was only noon. Barring any unforeseen difficulties, I'd be able to conclude my business with Don Faustino and make it back to Oaxaca City well before dark. Just as I had planned.

A dark, slender woman suddenly appeared in the doorway of the nearest shack. She waved uncertainly, then scurried like a squirrel down the path to greet me. Barefoot and pretty, her long black braided hair hanging down around her waist, Doña Elisia had the shining eyes and warm beatific smile of a saint, which, I was about to discover, she was not far from being.

"Don Faustino will be right back," she said brightly. "Please come in."

"He's not here?" For the second time in fifteen minutes I had asked a completely unnecessary question. It had to be the heat.

"He told me to tell you that there was a family emergency," she said serenely. "But not to worry. He won't be long."

Something in the way Doña Elisia had phrased her reply gave me a most unpleasant feeling. But the woman's beatific smile and child-like enthusiasm so disarmed me that I found myself nodding, smiling and following her obediently up to the shaded verandah where I was graciously ushered into the womb-like confines of an ancient armchair. Then my hostess scurried off, only to return several moments later with a tall glass of warm lemonade. I thanked her profusely as she flashed a dazzling smile, made a sort of curtsey and hurried away again.

The minute she was out of sight I dug out my water purification drops and dosed the lemonade. Then I sank down, down, down into the abyss of the armchair and began to wait.

It was hot in the shade of the verandah, but not hellishly so, and there were remarkably few flies. This entomological shortfall I attributed to the remarkable cleanliness of the ground around me which appeared to have been meticulously swept within the past fifteen minutes. And so it seemed a little odd when a young woman materialized with a broom and began to sweep the area immediately in front of the verandah.

The woman was twenty or so years old and appeared to be enjoying herself immensely. Every so often she would shoot me a furtive smile and begin to giggle. When I smiled politely back, she averted her gaze and giggled some more.

After a while, Doña Elisia returned with a plateful of rice, beans, scrambled eggs and tortillas.

"You haven't touched your lemonade yet," she chided me gently.

By now the drops had surely had sufficient time to slaughter every living thing in their vicinity, so I hoisted the glass and downed the entire contents in one long swallow, hoping to convince Doña Elisia that I was not just another paranoid gringo, which of course I was.

"This is my eldest daughter, Maria," Doña Elisia said, indicating the sweeper.

"How do you do?" I said.

"She's a widow," Doña Elisia said cheerfully. "Her husband was run over last year by a bus. "

"That's too bad," I said uncertainly.

Maria giggled, and kept right on sweeping.

Just as I was about to finish my lunch another young woman appeared and (like Carl Lewis preparing to anchor the four-by-one hundred relay) took the broom authoritatively from Maria's hand.

Simultaneously, Doña Elisia appeared at my elbow with a generous helping of homemade flan.

"This is my daughter, Esperanza," she chirped merrily.

Esperanza was not a giggler. Looking me boldly in the eye, she beamed in my direction a smile which could have melted stainless steel. Maria, now off-stage left somewhere, was very pretty, but Esperanza...Esperanza was shockingly, terrifyingly beautiful, and so obviously in heat... I attempted to say "*mucho gusto*" (nice to meet you), but my throat had gone dry, and only the "mu" came out, making me sound like a cow with Strepp throat. Then I felt myself blush, something I had not done for more than twenty years.

"Esperanza is seventeen years old," Doña Elisia informed me.

All at once it dawned on me: I was being presented with potential brides!

For just an instant I imagined myself married to Esperanza.

"Do-Do-Doña Elisia," I stammered, "do you think Don Faustino will be back soon?"

"Yes, at any moment," she replied without conviction.

I checked my watch. Time was running short.

"Doña Elisia," I said, trying desperately to keep my eyes off of her daughter's faultless, gently gyrating, loin-lathering behind, "do you think it would be possible to see the sculptures?"

"They're all locked up in Don Faustino's workshop," she replied.

"And you don't have the key."

"No," she said sadly, "Don Faustino has the only copy."

The remainder of the hot afternoon crawled inexorably by in a blur of sweeping young women and warm lemonade. By the time Don Faustino finally made his appearance, the ground in front of the verandah had been rendered totally devoid of soil, my eight prospective brides having swept right down to solid rock. And all hope of returning to Oaxaca before dark had, along with the soil, vanished as well.

"Compadre!" Don Faustino bellowed, locking me in a brief but fierce embrace.

"Don Faustino, where..."

"Mujer!" Don Faustino shouted, "bring me a chair."

"Don Faustino, I..."

"Sit down, sit down," he commanded.

"I've been sitting all..."

"Mujer!" Don Faustino ordered his wife, "bring us some mescal. The good stuff," he added, "not the crap we serve your brothers."

"Don Faustino, I don't..."

"Compadre!" he declared. "Only the best for my Compadre."

All of my protests—that I didn't drink mescal; that I was tired of sitting down; that I wanted to leave—were summarily ignored, like the desultory barking of the starving strays at Don Faustino's gate. So I returned to the armchair, accepted a glass of mescal and hoisted it high in the air, as the sculptor and I toasted each other's health.

"Salud!" Don Faustino exclaimed with violence.

"Salud," I said half-heartedly.

By the time we had concluded our second "salud", I was growing more than a little desperate to see my sculptures (in fact, I was beginning to doubt their existence altogether), so I suggested that we take a tour of his fabled workshop. Don Faustino brushed my suggestion aside, urging me instead to drink my mescal "like a man", instead of sipping it "like an old lady". After a bit of haggling, we reached a compromise: he would show me his taller as soon as I had belted back two full shots of his vintage moonshine.

Don Faustino was enormously proud of his taller, which was after all just another dirt-floor shack. The dozen pieces I had commissioned were all lined up on a high wobbly shelf. Every one of them was exquisitely done, picture-perfect. Except for the rabbit. Whereas the Texas-sized genitalia made a crude kind of aesthetic sense on the various pigs, bulls, burros and jaguars, on the rabbit they seemed somehow...inappropriate. When I pointed out this anomaly to Don Faustino, he reacted in the most violent fashion.

"It is a macho rabbit!" he shouted.

"Yes, Don Faustino, but..."

"It is a rabbit with balls!" he screamed.

"I can see that, but..."

"A rabbit has long ears, doesn't it?"

"Well, yes."

"So," he said with ineluctable logic, "why can't it have a long prick?"

Without any further discussion, I paid Don Faustino for the sculptures, which we packed up and loaded into my car. Then we returned to the veranda where we picked up exactly where we had left off. There being no alternative now, I came quickly to terms with my situation, with the fact that I would have to spend the night.

"Salud, Compadre!" I said with real enthusiasm.

"Salud!" he shouted back.

At peace now with my fate, my mood began to improve dramatically. Don Faustino's mescal was truly exceptional. Smooth, full-bodied and delicious, the liquor left me floating in a warm, soothing cloud of cactus-flavored euphoria, as my previously grim surroundings were miraculously transformed into a quaint and rustic wonderland. Even the prospect of being vivisected the following day by my wife no longer seemed to trouble me.

Time floated leisurely, affably by.

Blissfully savoring the liquid perfection of my fifth mescal, I felt a light tap upon my shoulder. It was Don

Faustino, regarding me with me a strange, expectant look. "Well?" he said.

"Well, what?"

"Well, how do you like them?" he asked, arching an eyebrow.

"They are truly magnificent," I replied expansively. Even the rabbit, I was prepared to agree, was a masterpiece of overstatement.

"And which is your favorite?"

"They're all so beautiful," I replied sincerely. "It's hard to say."

"*Por supuesto*," (of course) Don Faustino said impatiently, "but which is your favorite? You must have a favorite."

"I do?"

"*Por supuesto.* You can't marry them all, you greedy bastard."

"Oh."

"You just tell me which one you want, *hijo* (son). The Justice of the Peace will be arriving any minute."

"Don Faustino," I said, laughing, "we seem to have ourselves a small misunderstanding here. I'm already married."

"So?"

"So, I can't get married again."

"Why not?"

"Well, for one thing it's against the law."

"Big deal," Don Faustino said with contempt. "*La ley vale madre.*" (The law is worthless.)

"Right. Of course. So, how many wives do you have, Don Faustino?"

"Shhhhh!" he said. "Not so loud." Don Faustino stood up, slowly scanning the entire area. Then he sat down, looked me straight in the eye, and held up three fingers.

"You've got three wives?" I exclaimed.

Don Faustino smacked me painfully on the top of my head and warned me again to keep my voice down.

"So which is your favorite?" he insisted.

"Compadre," I said evasively, "there were so many I can't remember who was which."

"Correcto," Don Faustino grunted. "Mujer!"

When Doña Elisia appeared before us once again with her soft shining eyes and her patient saintly smile, Don Faustino made a circular motion with his forefinger, like a referee signaling the players that it was time to resume play. Doña Elisia nodded once and scurried away. Several minutes later two giggling young broom-bearing women shuffled shyly onto the veranda.

"No, not again," I moaned.

"What's the matter?"

"Nothing, Compadre, it's just that..."

"You're confused," Don Faustino offered.

"Well, yes."

"You can't keep track of who's who."

"Right."

"Correcto. Mujer!"

Don Faustino instructed his wife to bring us a pad of paper and a pen. When she had done so, he explained to me that we were going to go about this business in a "systematic and scientific manner".

Since there was absolutely no arguing with the man and because I was by now seriously drunk, I said, "Correcto. We'll give each prospect a number."

"Exactamente," Don Faustino grunted. "The one with the red dress is Rosa. The skinny one is Amparo."

"Number one and number two," I said, writing their names on my pad.

"Correcto," Don Faustino agreed.

"Exactamente," I said. "How old is Rosa?"

"How the hell should I know?" Don Faustino replied.

"Well, she's your daughter, isn't she?"

"No, she's my niece. Rosa, how old are you?"

"Fifteen," she replied shyly.

Oh, my God!

"And what are her favorite hobbies?" I asked.

"Hobbies?" Don Faustino did not seem to recognize the concept.

"Yeah, you know, what does she like to do?"

"Whatever you tell her, Compadre."

"No, no, no. I mean, what does she like to do in her spare time?"

"Spare time? Are you crazy? A woman has no spare time."

"Alright," I said. "What is she good at? Sewing? Embroidery?"

"Of course."

"What else?"

Don Faustino gave me a sly look and punched me playfully on the shoulder. "That you'll have to find out for yourself," he said.

"Correcto," I said. "Now, how old is Amparo?"

"Number two," Don Faustino said, reading from my pad. "Eighteen."

"Excelente," I said. "Who's next?"

"Mujer!"

The afternoon's second sweeping marathon ended just as the sun was setting behind the most distant tortured hillside. Don Faustino and I were sitting shoulder to shoulder in the dirt—for some besotted reason we had abandoned our chairs.

"Pues, mi hijo," Don Faustino said affectionately, "which one will it be?"

"Pues, papi," I replied with equal feeling, "let's review the panorama."

"You know," Don Faustino confessed, "I always wanted a son. Seven daughters. What rotten luck!"

"But you have wonderful daughters," I said. "You should be proud."

"It's my own fault," Don Faustino said, turning maudlin. "I'm no damn good. God is punishing me. I drink too much. I use foul language. I'm unfaithful to my wives."

"But you're a great artist," I said. "A man of talent. A man of respect!"

"I'm just a useless old fart," Don Faustino whined on. "No good to anything or anybody. They ought to shoot me—put me out of my misery, like the sick old dog I am." To my amazement, his badly bloodshot eyes began to fill with tears.

"Don Faustino," I said with drunken conviction, "I wish I was half the man you are."

"Half?"

"Yes, half!"

"Don't flatter yourself," Don Faustino said, his eyes drying at once. "If you were one tenth the man I am, it'd be a goddamn miracle!"

"Correcto."

"Vamos," Don Faustino said impatiently, "which one will it be?"

"Bueno," I said, picking up my notes. "Let's see. We have eight prospective brides here. Each one has been given a numerical rating from one to fifty. If you give me a few days, I'm positive I can make an intelligent decision."

"Alright, let's cut the crap," Don Faustino snarled at me.

"What do you mean?" I asked in alarm. The most venomously deranged expression had suddenly appeared on the sculptor's face.

"You and I both know," he said somberly, "that the issue has never been in doubt. We are both men. We both have eyes. We both have *pitos* (pricks). Mujer!"

"Si, Faustino?"

"Get Esperanza into that wedding dress. Rapido!"

Wait a minute, I wanted to scream, this game has gone too far! But the words just stuck to my tongue.

"Have another drink," Don Faustino said, passing me the bottle. "With any luck you'll be fertilizing the fields by nightfall."

Fertilizing the fields?

My eyes glazing rapidly over with shock, I took the bottle and put it to my lips. But just as I was about to swallow, Don Faustino, cackling like a madman, slapped me with all his strength on my back. Mescal sprayed from my mouth all over the veranda, and I was seized with a violent fit of choking.

"*Hijo mio*," Don Faustino roared, "*eres un gran puto, pero te quiero por todos modos.*" (My son, you're a tremendous faggot, but I love you anyway.)

Don Faustino was still laughing insanely, and I had just stopped choking, when a fat porcine-featured man wearing a sweat-soaked t-shirt and carrying an enormous ledger waddled, huffing and puffing, up to the veranda.

"Ah, right on time," Don Faustino snorted with satisfaction. "Mujer!"

Without even being asked, Doña Elisia deposited another folding chair on the veranda, and rushed off again.

"So, this must be your future son-in-law," the fat man said.

"Yes," Don Faustino said, putting his arm around my shoulders. "Hijo," he said to me, "this is Don Pedro, our Justice of the Peace."

"They're fucking insane, the whole lot of them," I muttered to myself in English.

"What? What's that he said?" the fat man asked.

"Speak Spanish to the man, hijo," Don Faustino commanded me. "Nobody here understands that gringo drivel."

"Mucho gusto," I told the fat man.

"So, where's the beautiful novia?" Don Pedro asked.

"She's getting dressed," Don Faustino said.

"Ah, very good, very good. And my, uh, fee?" Don Pedro asked coyly.

Don Faustino reached into his pants pocket, pulled out a wad of bills and held them under the fat man's nose. Don Pedro, his beady eyes aglow with greed, attempted to snatch them out of his hand, but Don Faustino was too quick for him. "After the ceremony is concluded," Don Faustino said, shoving the wad back into his pocket.

Having by now recovered from my initial shock, I took a large swallow of mescal to screw up my courage and said, "I'm not doing it."

Both men regarded me with looks of astonishment.

"I'm already married," I told Don Pedro. "Don Faustino is drunk, and so am I. We're both drunk," I added needlessly.

The fat man turned to Don Faustino. "Is this true?" he demanded.

"Yes, we're drunk," Don Faustino admitted. "So what? Where does it say you have to be sober to get married? I know I wasn't."

Don Pedro, mentally fingering the wad of bills, said, "Yes, I suppose that's true. There is no law with which I am familiar which states that one must be sober at the moment of matrimonial contraction."

"Didn't you hear what I just said!" I yelled at the fat man. "I'm already married. I have a wife. She's waiting for me back in Oaxaca in a hotel."

"I must say," Don Pedro said, "I do envy you. On what they pay me I could never afford to keep a wife in a hotel. By the way," he added thoughtfully, "is your wife—the one in the hotel—is she also a foreigner?"

"Yes, but…"

"Well then," Don Pedro said with judicial authority, "as I see it, what we have here is a clear-cut case of non-overlapping civil jurisdictions. Granted, the situation might be regarded by those of little legal acumen somewhat, uh, vaguely, um…However, in as much as this will be your first marriage to a Mexican national, at least in the state of Oaxaca, I do not see any compelling reasons why we cannot, utilizing articles 64 and 69 of the Constitution as our firm legal basis, proceed with the ceremony."

"Compelling reasons?" I shouted. "Compelling reasons! Here's a compelling reason, you fat, money-grubbing windbag: I'm not going to do it. You've got no groom. No groom: no marriage! Comprende?"

Don Pedro favored me with an ugly scowl, letting me know in no uncertain terms that he'd been deeply offended by my rude outburst. Meanwhile, for some mysterious reason, Don Faustino was as calm as could be. "We'll see," was all he said.

I took another slug of mescal and passed the bottle to Don Faustino. "There's nothing personal in this," I told my would-be father-in-law. "I feel a great affection for you. And Esperanza is a wonderful girl. (I gave her a fifty-plus, by the way.) The thing is, this is just an impossible situation—from an ethical standpoint."

"An ethical standpoint," Don Faustino repeated calmly, taking a long pull on the bottle. "Don't worry, hijo, everything will work out in the end."

Esperanza, followed by her mother and all of her sisters, made her grand entrance a moment later. She was wearing a full-blown wedding dress, which might have looked absurd there on the rustic veranda had it been worn by a normal girl. But Esperanza, glowing with animal-vigor and the kind of supernatural beauty seen only in the movies, was absolutely stunning. It required an act of enormous will just to tear my eyes off her.

Damn my eyes. What I really wanted to tear off at that moment was her dress.

Don Faustino, meanwhile, had called over one of his daughters and whispered something in her ear. The young girl, I think it was Elena (number six: 39 points), went running off. Then he stepped to my side and whispered in my ear. "Alright, you filthy gutless cabron. If you won't do it, you won't do it. But let's see what you're made of. Let's see you, out of respect, take Esperanza's hand, look her in the eye, and tell her you won't marry her. Let's see if at least you've got the balls to do that."

Don Faustino was truly a sly old bastard, I thought. Hold Esperanza's hand? Look into her eyes? Tell her no? God Almighty! Could I do it? In all honesty, I wasn't sure.

After a while I decided that I had better at least give it a try. "Alright," I said finally. "I'll tell her. But once I do, you have to promise to call this whole thing off, once and for all."

"You have my solemn word," Don Faustino said.

With the reluctance of a condemned man stumbling up to the gurney to receive his lethal injection, I walked unsteadily across the yard. Esperanza, phosphorescent with passion, held out her hand, and I took it in mine.

"Esperanza," I said, my voice a hoarse croak, "I have to tell you something. Never in my life have I known a girl as beautiful as you. You have the face of an angel, the body of…what I mean to say is, if things were different, if I wasn't already…"

"No!" someone screamed, as if in pain. "Over my dead body!"

All of us turned to stare with open-mouthed disbelief at the source of this anguished shout. From out of nowhere a stocky young campesino with the eyes of a maddened bull had charged into the garden brandishing a machete.

"It's Rodruigo," Don Faustino announced, as if he were narrating a play. "He is here to fight for the hand of my daughter." Before I could fully comprehend what was happening, the crazy old bastard had strode to my side and stuck a machete in my hand.

Dazed by the heat and the mescal, drained by the supreme effort of will it had required to deny myself Esperanza, instead of running for my life, I simply stood there like a fool with my mouth agape, holding the machete.

Everyone, including Esperanza, backed off to one side while Rodruigo strode with the lethal self-assurance of a jaguar to within five feet of where I was standing.

"As Esperanza's father," Don Faustino went on in his narrator's voice, "I have decided that whoever is left standing when the fight is over, will marry my daughter right here. On the spot."

"I'll kill you, you filthy gringo," Rodruigo spat at me. "I'll cut you to pieces." The young man began to circle, weaving the air with his machete.

"Don Faustino," I moaned, "this is insane. Tell him the truth. Tell him…"

"Stop whining and fight like a man!" Don Faustino instructed me.

Maybe this is all a joke, I thought desperately to myself, a little farce which Don Faustino has arranged for his own perverse entertainment. At any moment, the campesino will drop his machete and smile, and everyone will have a good laugh at my expense. But no. One look at the young man's face, contorted with loathing, rage and anguish, told me that this was not a joke, that there could be no doubt as to his intentions: he was about to slice me into little pieces!

I looked without hope at the machete hanging limply at my side. Only once in my life had I even held such an implement in my hand. It was back in Puerto Vallarta, in my front yard. I'd been trying to cut open a coconut. My pathetically inept blow had bounced sideways off of the coconut and opened up a deep gash in my leg.

Rodruigo began to dance around me in tight little circles, feinting, probing, closing in for the kill. I glanced with mounting terror all around me, willing someone to step forward and save me from this nightmare. Esperanza's eyes, I was less than pleased to see, were blazing with excitement and anticipation. Don Faustino was smirking with satisfaction. Don Pedro's beady little eyes were filled with fear—fear of losing his fee. Dona Elisia and the other women were staring at me with expressions of deep sorrow, as if I already lay wounded and bleeding on the ground.

"Fight, or don't fight," Rodruigo hissed at me. "Either way, you die!"

"Rodruigo," I said, backing away, "you can have her. I don't want to get married. This is all a big mistake."

"You lie!" Rodruigo said, taking one final step forward, raising his machete high into the air.

Finally, too late as it turned out, it dawned on me that my best course of action, under the circumstances, was to throw dignity to the wind and run for my life. I took a small step backwards, tensing my muscles for flight, and bumped up against the garden's barbed wire fence. All of the blood left my legs then as I steeled myself for the coming blow. My only hope was that it would miss a major artery.

"Wait!" Don Faustino shouted, stepping nimbly between us. Rodruigo just managed to stop his arm in mid-blow, the machete's blade halting within inches of Don Faustino's shoulder.

Putting his lips up against my ear, Don Faustino whispered, "This is your last chance. Swear you'll marry Esperanza and I'll call him off. Otherwise…"

Bigamy or death: what kind of choice was that? It was, even my wife would probably have to agree, no choice at all. "Okay, you win," I gasped. "I'll do it. I'll do it."

Don Faustino grunted and turned to Rodruigo. "I've changed my mind," he told the astonished youth. "The rich gringo marries Esperanza after all."

"What?" Rodruigo cried. "But, but, you said…"

"How many times do I have to tell you," Don Faustino said cruelly, "Esperanza is a rare gem, and you're just a common turd. You're not good enough for her, and never will be. Now go home. Get out of here. Scat!"

"I'll kill myself," Rodruigo said. "If she marries the gringo, I'll kill myself!"

"Fine," Don Faustino said, "just do it someplace else. Go on, get out of here. Before I lose my temper."

Without another word, the devastated Rodruigo, after casting one last pitiful glance back at Esperanza, shuffled miserably out of the garden.

Esperanza and I stood side-by-side holding hands as the ceremony began. Don Faustino had dressed me in a bright pink guayaberra shirt, which was several sizes too small for me. I'm sure I looked ridiculous in it, but I was much too far-gone to care. Dazed and confused to an extent unprecedented in all my adult life, my mind skittered wildly hither and yon, prey to a numbing stew of conflicting emotions. One moment I was consumed with hatred for Don Faustino and his demented machinations. The next, all I could feel were waves of pure relief at having escaped unmaimed my encounter with Rodruigo. Then it was shame's turn to wrack my heart with remorse over my sad display of cowardice. Shame led naturally to guilt: slice the cake any way you wished, I was about to betray my wife, the woman I loved. And thoughts of love and betrayal led finally, inexorably to...Esperanza.

As the fat Justice of the Peace droned on and on, the platitudes dripping from his mouth like drops of rancid grease from a leaky pan, all of those emotions continued to war for supremacy within my confused and battered breast. But then, gradually, as the ceremony drew to a close, one feeling, one hormone driven sentiment marched triumphantly to the fore. And it was, I am ashamed to say, the most ignoble of them all.

"You may kiss the bride," Don Pedro said, and as if he had uttered some magical incantation, I felt myself suddenly consumed with the most intense, undiluted passion imaginable for the child-goddess I now gathered franticly, desperately into my arms.

It was fully dark and a lovely crescent moon had climbed high over the eastern horizon as the fat Justice of the Peace opened the huge ledger so that Esperanza and I could sign our names, making my act of perfidy official. My hand shook so badly as I held the pen, I could hardly recognize my own signature. But there it was. I downed two quick shots of mescal, and told myself that none of this was my fault, that what was done was done, that I might as well make the best of a bad situation.

An indecently short time later, Don Faustino took me aside and indicated that the "matrimonial chamber" was ready and waiting, and that it was time I got down to business.

"I want this marriage consummated before midnight," he told me firmly.

"Correcto," I told my father-in-law.

"I want those sheets bloodied by dawn," he said, in case I had not understood him the first time.

"Exactamente," I replied.

When we were finally alone, Esperanza did not, as I had expected, put out the dim lamp which lit our humble room. But she did ask me, with trembling voice, to turn my back while she removed her dress. Stripped of her brash self-confidence, I saw Esperanza at that moment for what she truly was: an innocent seventeen-year-old virgin teetering on the brink of life's first abyss. This realization, which should have shamed me to the bone, only excited me the more. Scruples? I had left them to nature's truly monogamous creatures: the coyote, the jackal and the wolf—I was a man!

In an instant I had torn off my own clothes, and then we were in bed together, naked.

I will not even attempt to describe Esperanza without her clothes, except to say that she was perfect, everywhere and in every way. History's greatest sculptor, or artist or poet could not have improved upon the loveliness of her form, not in marble, not on canvas, not in their most exalted visions. We set upon each other with a ferocity, with a hunger I had never known.

The preliminaries lasted...how long I could not say. And then, the moment of (as Don Faustino had put it) consummation, was upon us. Time to put the exclamation point to our sentence of love. But when that critical moment arrived, my manhood, the pride of Jalisco, had inexplicably taken a hike. Suddenly, I was horseless, unarmed, defanged...in a word: *incapable*. Esperanza was shattered, assuming in her inexperience that my incapacity must somehow be her fault. After several more minutes of frantic, fruitless writhing, I was seized by an abrupt and irresistible wave of nausea. Before I could take evasive action, I had added insult to injury and thrown up—all over my new bride's peerless breasts.

I awoke the next morning just before dawn to the sound of a woman sobbing her heart out somewhere nearby. With an enormous effort I struggled to my knees, ignoring as best I could the hatchet, which someone had buried in the top of my skull. Crawling about blindly on the floor I found my pants and the pink guayaberra shirt. My shoes seemed to have disappeared. On my hands and knees, fighting back wave upon wave of nausea, I scrambled, barefoot, to the door.

Once outside, it took several moments to bring into focus the scene which awaited me there in the dim early morning light: Esperanza stood in the center of the garden, sobbing uncontrollably as she clung to her mother's neck. Don Faustino and the rest of the family stood off to one side, confused expressions on their sleep-stained faces. Against all odds, I climbed painfully to my feet. Esperanza looked up, saw me and rushed, still crying hysterically, to join her sisters. Don Faustino, who looked more dead than alive himself, staggered over to his wife, where he received from Doña Elisia's troubled lips an account of the night's anti-climactic events. At least I assumed he did, for the next moment he flew into an insane rage. Picking up the nearest thing to hand (a broom, naturally), he lunged at me, swinging wildly at my head and screeching the following:

"Pinche puto gringo! I should have known. *Joto sin ouevos! Maricon!*"

Several of his wild blows caught me on the arms and shoulders. I felt a fleeting urge to explain to Don Faustino that I was not a maricon, that it was the mescal which had done me in. But then, realizing that now was the perfect time to do what I should have done all along, I took to my bare heels and fled.

With my bride and all of my in-laws looking on, silent witnesses to the final act of my complete humiliation, I reached the gate, and fumbled at the latch, Don Faustino's weak but painful blows raining down on my unprotected back. Finally, I managed to open the gate and squeeze through, tearing the guayaberra shirt as well as my arm on the rusty wire.

Don Faustino chased me all the way to my car, holding the broom at port arms. Once I was inside and had started the engine, he proceeded to beat on the hood with the broom handle, shouting, "Hijo de la chingada!" over and over again.

Just as I cleared the square, still half-blind, driving by instinct alone, I thought I saw out of the corner of my eye, in front of a small dusty shack, Rodruigo's limp body hanging by its twisted neck from a dead jacaranda tree. I probably screamed. But I can't remember. I can, in fact, remember little of that long drive back to Oaxaca, except for the pain.

When finally I staggered, filthy, shoeless and smelling like a week-old corpse, into the lobby of the charming Hotel Colonial in downtown Oaxaca, it was only by one last heroic act of will that I was able to maintain an upright posture. For some unknown reason I was carrying the wooden rabbit, cradling it my arms on its back like a baby. As I wove my way to the reception desk, the clerk, an officious little twerp with whom I did not get along, was deep in conversation with a pair of nuns who were apparently in the process of checking-in.

"Is my wife in?" I asked in a hoarse voice.

The clerk cocked his head slightly and regarded me with disgust, as if I were a particularly large and hearty cockroach who had somehow managed to survive the morning's fumigation. The older of the two nuns turned to face me as well, her severe eyes locking on the rabbit's Herculean phallus which, at the moment, was pointing directly at her nose. Ignoring me with a studied disdain, the clerk returned his attention to the nuns, both of whom were now staring wide-eyed at the rabbit.

"Overlooking the pool, or the square?" the clerk asked the nuns.

The Sisters did not appear to hear him, so intent were they on glaring with zealous indignation first at the rabbit, and then at me.

"It's a macho rabbit," I felt compelled to explain.

"Did you speak?" the clerk asked me.

"My wife!" I growled ferociously. "Room 224! Is she in or not?"

"Yes, I believe she is in," he said, eyeing me warily now.

The nuns crossed themselves as I lurched towards the elevator.

"Oh my God!" my wife cried. "Are you all right? What happened? Were you robbed? What did they take?"

"Just my dignity," I said wearily. "Don't worry. I'm okay. Really."

"You don't look okay," she said with concern. "You look like shit."

"Thanks."

"Are you hungry?"

"No, no. I just need a hot bath and a few Percodans. I'll be fine."

My wife allowed me to lie in the tub unmolested for almost an hour. The hot water and the narcotics had by then restored me somewhat and I felt hopeful that I could deal with her inevitable questions.

"The sculptures are all wonderful," I told her. "Except for the rabbit. There may be a problem with the rabbit."

"I love the rabbit," she said. "So, what was it like?"

"What was what like?"

"The whole trip? How was it?"

"All and all," I replied, "it was a deeply humbling experience."

"And the road was pretty bad?"

"The worst," I said.

"No wonder you couldn't make it there and back the same day," she said.

I said nothing.

"And you drank too much mescal?"

"Far too much mescal," I replied.

"How did you get all those bruises?" she asked. "You look like you fell off a roof."

"I may have," I said evasively, "It's hard to remember."

"So, what else happened?" my wife demanded. She was, I could see, becoming impatient with my vague replies to her questions.

I had never once in all our years of marriage lied about anything of consequence to my wife. After praying silently for guidance to Santa Maria de Los Cielos, I decided that now was not the time to blemish my perfect record.

"Well, let's see," I said in my most off-hand manner. "After being served a delicious breakfast of scrambled eggs, rice and beans, I was given my pick of seven and a half lovely young virgins, the most beautiful of which I eventually married. But not until after I had nearly been maimed by her insanely jealous machete-wielding boyfriend, who, I'm fairly certain (but not positive—I may have been hallucinating) committed suicide by hanging himself from a dead jacaranda tree. Suicide is never a smart choice, but it was a particularly dumb thing to do in his case (if in fact he did do it) because, as it turned out, when push finally came to shove, I was too drunk to consummate the marriage, and if he'd only been a little more patient, he probably could have grabbed her on the rebound."

"What's a half a virgin?" my wife asked, smiling at what she took to be my habitually sick sense of humor.

"She was only half a virgin," I replied, quoting my father-in-law, "'because her brainless *pendejo* husband barely had time to break her in before the pitiful moron was run over by a slow-moving bus.'"

Mixed Blessings

My wife, normally a stand-by-your-man type of woman, had locked herself in the bedroom with a Vanity Fair and a pitcher of margaritas. She hadn't spoken a word to me in more than twelve hours, ever since I had lied to the Padre.

Rosa, our ex-maid, had planted herself like a short stout shrub in the garden, where she stood quivering like a hibiscus bush in the breeze.

"Rosa, come inside," I pleaded.

"Not until the Padre arrives." Rosa stared fearfully at the ground between her feet, as if at any moment she expected the ground to open up and swallow her.

This left me only Sombra and Negra, our badly spoiled house cats, for company. Sombra had caught a fair sized iguana earlier that morning and now sat at my feet making nauseating little crunching noises as she reduced the reptile's muscular hindquarters to kitty-sized chunks. Negra, from her perch atop the terminally cluttered dining room table, looked anxiously on.

"That looks pretty tasty," I said to Sombra. "But don't be a pig. Leave some for your sister." The cats, like all the other females in my immediate proximity, ignored me.

By the time the Padre arrived, four shots of Raicilla later, I was in such an altered state that I failed to recognize him—an unpardonable sin since I had just seen him the day before. Of course, it was not entirely my fault; without his vestments he looked so normal; in fact, he looked exactly like a door-to-door salesman. We'd had an outbreak of them lately, along with dengue bearing mosquitoes—they both seemed to proliferate with the onset of the rains.

The Padre was small, plump and dainty. His expression was one of distressed impatience, which along with his pointy nose and matching ears, gave him the look of an over-fed Chihuahua in urgent need of a utility pole.

Just what I need, I thought grimly as I opened the door, someone trying to shove dust-busters down my throat. "Whatever it is you're selling," I said rudely, "I don't need it."

The Padre's face clouded with confusion. "I'm not selling anything," he said.

"You've got that right," I said. "So why don't you take your vacuum-cleaners and your hair brushes and your herbal suppositories, and whatever else you've got in that bag and go pester some other sucker."

"Have you been drinking?" the Padre asked.

"Not enough to put up with this crap," I said. "Listen, pal, there's a Padre on his way over here right now for a really big blessing, so even if I was stupid enough to buy the garbage you're peddling, I don't have the time. Comprende?"

"But I *am* the Padre!" the small man yipped at me.

"Oh."

There are two basic universally accepted rationales for having your house blessed: either it is a new home, or else someone has just died in it. I had an altogether different motive, and it was anything but basic. It involved Rosa, our ex-maid.

Sweet nervous Rosa had stood in our kitchen a week earlier and with downcast eyes informed my wife and I that she was giving notice, that this would be her last day. Naturally, we were devastated. We loved Rosa. She'd been with us for fifteen years. She was loyal, honest, efficient and conscientious. Over the years we had come to rely on Rosa so completely that we had become, for all intents and purposes, helpless.

"But why?" we yelled in unison.

"It's my Bruja," Rosa said with tears in her eyes. "She told me I have to quit. For my personal safety."

Bruja, if you go simply by the dictionary, means, *witch*. But in Mexico, the world's most ambiguous country, a Bruja can be almost anything: fortuneteller, investment adviser, healer, psychologist, detective, evil sorceress, etc.

Rosa's Bruja had no particular specialty, making her a kind of Family Bruja or General Practitioner. Rosa had sought the woman out after suffering several fainting spells, which no doctor could account for, while cleaning the shower stall in our guest bathroom.

"So what exactly did the Bruja tell you, Rosa?" I asked.

Rosa's reply was confused, disjointed and rambling, but what it came down to was this: *aliens* were, according to the Bruja, attempting to communicate with Rosa in our guest bathroom, and somehow these otherworldly transmissions were upsetting Rosa's mental equilibrium to the point of making her momentarily lose consciousness.

But why *her*, we wanted to know. And why *our* guest-bathroom? And who *were* these aliens, anyway?

These were questions to which the Bruja, unlike Carl Jung, apparently had no answers. All the Witch knew for certain was that if Rosa did not change employers at once, the fainting spells would quickly graduate to Grand Mal seizures, which would in turn lead to possible paralysis as well as the loss of most of her teeth. To avoid this grim fate, all Rosa had to do was quit her job and sprinkle herself three times a day (before meals) with an expensive brownish powder, which looked suspiciously like dirt.

"Rosa, you're pulling my leg," I said.

"No," Rosa replied, "this is no joke. I have to leave right now. I can't even stay to wash the dishes."

Had my doctor, in the course of a routine exam, informed me that I needed to have my nose removed, I could not have been more shocked.

It had been fifteen years since I had last washed a dish and I seemed to recall that the procedure involved soap, water and some type of friction producing device, but beyond that it was all just a painful blur. But then I was a man, by definition, helpless. I turned desperately to my wife. Even after twenty years of living in Mexico, where no task is too trivial to pay someone else to do, the odds were that my wife still retained one or two of her genetically imprinted domestic instincts.

"Lucy," I said cautiously, "do you think you could, you know"—I pointed with my chin at the kitchen sink.

By way of reply my wife held out her recently manicured nails, and looked at me as if I was insane.

Aside from the fact that Rosa was in every way the ideal maid, forgetting for the moment the undiluted pain of losing her after fifteen blissfully spoiled and slothful years, what disturbed me the most was the terrible knowledge of how difficult it would be to replace her.

My wife had met Rosa in the ladies room of the Gustavo Diaz Ordaz International Airport in Puerto Vallarta where she was cheerfully mopping the floor. Both of the women were gregarious by nature and they quickly struck up a conversation. Lucy soon learned that Rosa worked forty-eight hours a week cleaning the bathrooms in the airport for what amounted to slave wages. My wife, knowing a gem when she met one, made Rosa an offer she could not refuse: working *only twenty-four hours a week,* cleaning *a beautiful house on the beach,* and making *the same slave wages she was making now*!

Prior to contracting Rosa we had gone through five different maids in two months.

Our first maid, Erigaberta, only lasted three days. She was a massively unattractive, mustachioed woman built like a small bull. And though she would never win a beauty contest, except possibly at a state fair, it was her interior lack of grace which drove us to cut her, as it were, so rapidly from the herd.

Erigaberta was unbelievably negative, a pessimist's pessimist, uncannily adept at finding the gray cloud surrounding any silver lining. On her second morning, while she was crushing my dress shorts into submission with fierce furious strokes of the iron, I made the mistake of attempting to lighten her leaden mood.

"Erigaberta," I said, "just look out the window at that beautiful blue ocean and those marvelous green mountains. Are we not indeed fortunate to live in such a wonderful place?"

Erigaberta looked up from my brutalized shorts, glared at the choppy water and said in her deep doomsday voice, "The Ocean is angry. You should move out of this house before we're all buried by a giant wave."

"But, Erigaberta," I said reasonably, "no wave has even come near this house for thirty years."

"That's what I mean," she grumbled, "the odds are against us."

"What Erigaberta needs," my wife told me later that day, "is a good vibrator."

"Right. I'll suggest it to her next employer."

Our second maid, Luz Maria, was a good worker, punctual, efficient and positive. Unfortunately, what she was most positive of was that I should divorce my wife and marry her nineteen-year-old daughter. Naturally, I told her that I was happily married and would prefer to drop the whole subject.

"But she's too old for you," Luz Maria kept telling me.

"She's exactly my age," I replied.

"That's what I mean," she said. "You need someone younger."

"Like your daughter?"

"Yes. Why not?"

This went on for several weeks. Then one day she brought her daughter along to work. My wife *happened* to be out of town for the day, and I was laid-up in bed with a bad back. When the daughter, who was far from unattractive, began to mop the floor in my bedroom, the pain in my back suddenly vanished. She had the most curious mopping technique. While the mop itself hardly seemed to move, her deliciously molded nineteen-year-old derriere was everywhere at once: rising, dipping, going in, going out. And as she danced erotically around the room her eyes never left my face, an expression of intense longing...

"Go get your mother," I told her finally.

"She went to the market," the girl replied. "She won't be back for at least an hour. "Is something wrong? Do you want a massage?"

When Luz Maria returned from the market, I should have fired her right there on the spot. But somehow I couldn't bring myself to do it—her ironing was *that* good. So in the evening I recounted the entire incident to my wife who had no problem whatsoever giving her the ax the following morning.

Our third maid was almost ideal. Her only fault was an unreasoning fear of my museum-quality collection of Michoacan Devil Masks, for which I had grossly over-paid and which I had been attempting to pawn off on some unsuspecting tourist ever since. After one week of working in a continual state of blind terror, she quit.

Maid number four hated cats. We had to let her go when we caught her attempting to stuff our orange tabby into the freezer compartment of the refrigerator. "It hissed at me," she claimed.

Maid number five was a hard working, clean, efficient woman in her early forties. Her only flaw was that she was a nymphomaniac with a particular passion for bus drivers. One day we came home unexpectedly and found her in our bed with a driver from the Estrella Blanca line. While my wife was in the process of letting her go, she confessed that all professional drivers drove her wild: bus drivers, taxi drivers, truck drivers—but especially bus drivers. She wasn't certain, but thought it might have something to do with those long gear sticks.

"That's very interesting," Lucy told her. "You're fired."

One thing you learn quickly when living in the tropics is the importance of keeping your house clean and tidy. Microbes, fungi, insects and vermin are all inordinately fond of the warm moist climate and reproduce with phenomenal gusto. And so it was not surprising that after five days of total neglect our house had begun to take on a somewhat fetid air, like the crime scene in one of those movies where the victim's body is not discovered until weeks or even months after the heinous act is committed.

On that critical sixth morning my wife and I found ourselves standing before the kitchen sink staring glassy-eyed at the awesome pile of crud-encrusted dishes. Like the veteran detective in the movie, I was managing with only a scented handkerchief. My wife, on the other hand, like the unseasoned rookie, was experiencing considerable difficulty.

"I guess we're going out for breakfast again," she said in a shell-shocked monotone.

"You know," I said through the handkerchief, "if they ever built a theme park for cockroaches, I bet it would look just like our sink."

"On second thought," she said as she turned a more vivid shade of green, "let's skip breakfast and go find a priest."

Lucy was not being facetious. Rosa, when pressed by us to name a circumstance under which she might reconsider her decision, had mentioned the possibility of having the house blessed by the Padre. If the house were blessed, Rosa felt, the aliens might go away. We had, at the time, laughed out loud at this patent piece of absurdity. We weren't laughing any longer.

Finding a Padre to bless the house should have been a relatively simple matter, but it was not.

The Padres at the main Guadalupe Cathedral were so up to their collars in baptisms, marriages, deaths and confessions, we couldn't even get an interview. So we headed for one of Vallarta's second-tier churches and asked to see the Padre there.

As it turned out, there were two Padres in residence and one of them consented to see us immediately. Seated behind his desk in the Rectory, the Padre, who must have seen one too many Pat O'Brien movies, actually said, "How can I help you, my children?"

"We want to have our house blessed," I said.

"And why is that?" The Padre inquired kindly.

My wife, being the only Catholic in the family, took the initiative and replied. And against my better judgment, she told the truth.

"So," the Padre said after a moment's meditation. "Essentially, the reason is that your maid is afraid of spirits or aliens or some such nonsense."

"Yes," my wife said.

"Well," the Padre shrugged, "that's her problem."

"But Padre," I broke in, "if she is troubled in spirit, doesn't that make it the Church's problem, too?"

"Not necessarily," he replied.

The next moment a woman rushed in and called the Padre away on urgent business. But he was quickly replaced by the other Padre, who stepped briskly into the Rectory and asked us if he could be of assistance.

This Padre was much younger and even more sympathetic than his predecessor.

"I'm Padre Mario," he said, firing up a Marlboro, and in so doing, exposing a thick gold bracelet on his wrist.

Padre Mario had grown himself a fairly respectable mustache and, at least from an ecclesiastical point of view, was probably in need of a haircut. He also spoke perfect idiomatic English and, though I am no expert, appeared to be wearing his collar at an unorthodoxically rakish angle. I had read somewhere that the Church was concerned about its inability to "connect" with today's young people. Padre Mario must have been anointed with that failing in mind.

"You guys are from the States, aren't you?" he asked in his disconcertingly excellent English.

"Yes, " I replied in the same language.

" Far out," he said. "I went to college in Wisconsin. Boy, that was cold! The inferno? Forget about it. You want Hell, man, try spending the winter in Madison."

This Padre Mario is pretty hip, I thought to myself. Maybe I should offer him a joint.

"We need to have our house blessed," my wife said.

"Right on. I can handle that," Padre Mario said. "Where do you live?"

I told him.

"Sorry, dude, no can do," he said, lighting up a second Marlboro from the butt of the first.

"Why not?"

"Hey, don't get me wrong. I'd love to help you out. But you're like, you know, in the wrong parish."

The right parish, it so transpired, was behind the stadium. On the way over there, my wife and I became entangled in a small argument.

"Let me do the talking this time," I told her.

"Why?" she asked. "What are you going to say?"

"I'm going to lie," I said.

"To a Priest?"

"Yes."

"Not with me there," she said.

"Fine."

"What are you going to tell him? It's my house, too. I have a right to know."

"I'm going to tell him what he wants to hear," I said, "that someone died."

"Someone *died*?"

"That's right."

"But who?"

"I haven't decided yet."

"Take me home."

After taking my wife home, I drove over to the San Miguel Church, which was located halfway between the municipal stadium and the municipal slaughterhouse.

Except for a solitary crone all bundled-up in black, the church was deserted.

Over the years I'd been in hundreds of Mexican churches, and all of them had contained at least one of these ancient over-dressed women. Apparently, they were all widows and they all looked exactly alike, as if they'd been processed in some great solitary crone-cloning factory. Even when more than one occupied the same church at the same time, they usually sat far apart, unwilling to recognize each other's existence, living monuments to Solitary Suffering.

This particular crone, who had a bottle of *Vidrio Express* (the Mexican version of *Windex*) in one hand and some wadded-up newspaper in the other, was attempting to clean a rectangular glass case inside of which was a regulation life-size statue of Jesus Christ laying contentedly on his back.

Like the crones, these saint-cases were strictly standard issue. I'd seen them in churches from Chihuahua to Chiapas. But they still made me nervous. Lying in their glass boxes, dressed in real clothing and painted with an eerie realism, the statues were a little too lifelike to suit me. I always expected one of them to start bleeding, or to sit up suddenly and ask for his money back.

Approaching the tiny old woman and interrupting her in mid-spritz, I asked for the Padre. Padre Pedro, she informed me, was taking his siesta.

"But I can wake him if it is urgent," she croaked helpfully.

Urgent? Before my inner eye I could clearly see the roaches occupying my kitchen sink. They were organizing themselves into unions, political parties and soccer teams. Eventually, the PRCI (*Partido Revolucionario de Cucarachas Institucional*) would win the popular vote, form a city council and enact legislation banning refuse removal, except during Lent.

On the other hand, disturbing the Padre's nap would probably not be wise.

"I'll wait," I said.

An hour later I was summoned to the Rectory. Padre Pedro, a small, chubby nondescript man, sat at his desk looking dazed and out of sorts, like a hairless bear coming out of hibernation.

"Padre," I said earnestly, "I need to have my house blessed."

"And why is that?" he inquired.

"Someone has died," I said somberly.

"A relative?"

"No, a neighbor."

My neighbor, although he had not died recently, *was* over eighty years old and, one had to assume, perfectly capable of dropping dead at any moment.

"Was there an accident?" the nosy Padre wanted to know.

"No," I said, "he died of natural causes. He was over eighty years old," I added, just to say something which was more or less true.

"I see," the Padre said. "So why exactly is it you feel you should have your house blessed?"

This was a question for which I was not prepared. I had assumed that a death in one's home automatically qualified the house, ipso facto, for a blessing.

"Well," I said, ad-libbing desperately, "I thought that in cases such as these when there is, how shall I put it, some confusion as to the precise nature of the expiration, it is more or less standard procedure to, ah, have the premises blessed."

"Confusion?" the Padre said. "I thought you said your neighbor died of natural causes."

"Yes, of course," I said. "Natural, but, um, unknown."

"Unknown natural causes?" Padre Pedro said doubtfully.

"Yes. Basically, uh, yes."

"I'm sorry, I don't understand," Padre Pedro said.

"Well, Padre," I said, "it's just so unsettling; the mystery of it all; the unexplained, unresolved aspects of the case, which become so much more disquieting when—how shall

I put it—an incomplete grasp of the spiritual, as opposed to, shall we say, the quotidian linear reality is involved."

"Yes, I see," the Padre said. But it was all too clear that what he was seeing was a deranged and babbling gringo who had disturbed his siesta and who he was about to throw out of his Rectory. It was time for desperate measures.

"By the way, Padre," I said casually, "not to change the subject, but I couldn't help but notice that the door to the church is in pretty bad shape. I know this must be a poor parish and I'd feel honored if I could make a small contribution towards its repair."

"Thank you. That's very generous," the Padre said.

"Don't mention it," I said.

"Would tomorrow at around noon be convenient?" he asked.

"Well, gosh, Padre, I've got my checkbook on me right now. Why wait till tomorrow? Or would you prefer cash?" I added quickly.

"I meant, for the blessing of your house," the Padre said.

On my way home I became so immersed in guilt over having lied to the Padre that I accidentally ran a red light. Unfortunately, a patrol car was right behind me (also running the red light) and I was quickly pulled over.

It had been several years since I had last bribed a policeman and frankly I was a little rusty. But bribing policemen, like riding a bicycle, is something you never really forget how to do. And so, after twenty minutes of intense negotiations we agreed upon a suitable sum and I was sent cheerfully, professionally and courteously upon my way.

Only later did it occur to me that I had, in only a thirty minute span, bribed both a priest and a policeman.

"If this keeps up," I told my wife over dinner, "they'll have to make me an honorary citizen."

My wife was not amused. "Shut up and eat your broccoli," she said.

Padre Pedro's arrival had thrown me into a veritable sea food soup of conflicting emotions. Failing to recognize him in his street clothes had been a poor beginning, and the fact that the entire procedure was to be carried out under false pretenses had left me, despite my lack of religious convictions, with a remorseful taste in my mouth. But most of all I was terrified that the blessing would not go well and that Rosa would, therefore, not wish to reclaim her job.

As I presented the Padre to Rosa and Lucy, he nodded perfunctory greetings and began to empty the contents of his shopping bag onto the only chair in the living room not encumbered with clothes, towels, old newspapers or reptilian body parts. The bag contained the Padre's vestments, which he hurriedly put on over his clothes.

"Where exactly did the deceased expire?" he asked without preamble. It was obvious he wanted to get this over with as quickly as possible, door or no door.

"Someone expired?" Rosa asked, her voice quaking with fear.

"Not yet," my wife said under her breath, casting a murderous glance my way.

"Right over here, Padre," I said, leading him directly to the guest bathroom.

Once we were inside I whispered, "Listen, Padre, let's not mention the word 'death' in front of my maid, please. She's very..."

"Very what?"

"Um, impressionable," I said lamely.

"There's something peculiar going on here, isn't there?" the Padre asked with suspicion.

"No, no," I said nervously, "nothing peculiar. Everything's perfectly normal. You know, death, life, living, dying. What could be more natural? First you live. Then you..."

"That's all right," Padre Pedro said, interrupting me, "just calm down. So, it was in here that he died?" he asked, producing a small flask of Holy Water from the pocket of his robe.

"Who died?" I heard Rosa whisper urgently to my wife from just outside the doorway.

"Yes, ah, basically," I replied, wishing I had laid off the Raicilla.

"Basically?"

I clamped my lips shut and nodded my head.

"Might I ask?" the Padre said, "where precisely your neighbor was at the moment of…"

This was not an easy question to answer. No one, as far as I knew, died standing up. And laying down in a bathroom (there was no tub, only a shower stall) seemed somehow inappropriate. Which left only one viable candidate. With a somber movement of my chin I indicated the general vicinity of the toilet.

"So, he was…" the Padre began.

"Yes, I'm afraid so. You know what they say, Padre: after a certain age every bowel movement becomes an adventure."

"Or a blessing," the Padre said knowingly, as he favored me for the first time in our acquaintance with a small smile.

Without any further ado the Padre began to sprinkle Holy Water all over the guest bathroom, reciting the usual Latin phrases and, I was pleased to see, giving preferential treatment to the W. C. Finally, with a last splash of Divine Moisture and a few "Dictum Pro Bonos", the Padre pronounced the blessing to be complete.

"What about the other bathroom?" Rosa asked from the doorway.

Unbeknownst to me, the Bruja had, on her third visit, communicated to Rosa her lack of certainty as to which of our two bathrooms was indeed the actual receptive terminus for the aliens' obnoxious transmissions. It was as if, the Bruja had explained to her client, the aliens were calling, not person-to-person, but rather, station-to-station.

"Padre," I said, "do you think it would be possible to bless the other bathroom as well?"

"What for?" he asked impatiently. "I thought he died in here."

"Well," I mumbled, "there was some confusion about that."

"What?" the Padre demanded. "Speak up."

"*Who died*?" Rosa asked my wife.

"Shhh!" Lucy said.

"Well," I began painfully, "we know for sure that the expiration took place in a bathroom. But since there are two bathrooms, perhaps the wisest course would be..."

"I don't understand," Padre Pedro interrupted me. "If the man died in this bathroom, what does the other bathroom have to do with it? He couldn't have died in both bathrooms."

"Well, Padre," I said humbly, "I'm sure you would know more about that than I would. However, for the sake of thoroughness, don't you think we could bless the other bathroom as well. Por favor?"

With the greatest reluctance, Padre Pedro followed me to the other bathroom where he splattered more Holy Water and mumbled more Latin. Meanwhile, my wife had grabbed my arm and dragged me off into a corner of our bedroom.

"Rosa wants him to bless your mask collection," she whispered to me urgently.

"Bless the Michoacan Devil Masks!" I hissed back at her. "Is she insane?"

"She's always been afraid of them," Lucy explained. "She says if he doesn't bless them she won't come back to work."

"Jesus Christ!" I moaned.

"Also," Lucy added maliciously, "she wants to know who died."

I told her to take Rosa back into the living room and wait for us there. Meanwhile, the Padre had begun to remove his vestments.

"No, wait!" I said frantically.

The Padre stopped and eyed me with displeasure. Too late it dawned upon me that it was not proper protocol for a layperson to give a Padre a direct order. "I'm sorry, Padre. Please forgive me."

"That's God's job," he replied coolly, "I'm only a priest."

"It's Rosa," I said.

"Rosa?" the Padre said. "Your maid? The woman who keeps asking who died?"

"Yes, her," I said breathlessly. "She's living in mortal fear."

"Of what?" The Padre, clearly fed-up with the entire business now, regarded me with a look which was anything but Christian.

"My museum quality collection of rare Mexican artifacts." I said, trying desperately to be as vague as possible.

"You mean the devil masks?" the Padre said with disgust.

"She's terrified, Padre. She says that unless they're blessed she can't work for us any more."

"Then let her find another job," the Padre said unhelpfully.

"But we don't want her to leave."

"Why not? She can't be a very good maid. Your house, if you'll excuse me saying so, is a mess."

"I know," I said, lying desperately. "That's why no one else will hire her. We only keep her on as an act of charity. She has nine children, you see, and no husband—he was run over by a bus. We love her like a daughter, Padre. If you could only do this one last thing. I implore you. *Por favor!*"

As the Padre stared at me his expression softened somewhat. I must have appeared more than a little pathetic to him, begging and pleading there in the ruins of my bedroom. Perhaps he even thought that I was a little crazy. And perhaps I was. In any case he nodded with resignation and said, "Alright. I'll bless the masks. But then I have to go."

As we exited the bedroom Negra and Sombra, made skittish by all of the unusual activity, ran between the Padre's feet, startling the poor man and causing him to stumble.

"Negra! Sombra! Cut that out!" I chided the felines.

"Those are your cats' names?" the Padre asked, surprised.

The Padre was surprised because both of the cats were totally white. I toyed briefly with the idea of explaining to him that naming a pair of white cats "Blackie" and "Shadow" was just my way of poking a little fun at the predictable names people often gave to their pets.

"It sounds better in English," I said instead.

The Padre said nothing, but stared at me for a long moment with concern.

Back in our beam-ceilinged living room, with its extraordinary display of rare and collectable Michoacan Devil Masks, Rosa and my wife were in the midst of a heated exchange.

"But then, why does he keep saying someone died?" Rosa demanded.

"I'll tell you later," Lucy replied.

"I want to know now," Rosa insisted.

When the Padre and I entered the room, the women fell silent. The Padre, checking to make sure he still had an adequate supply of Holy Water, began to approach the masks. But then, for no apparent reason, he stopped, well short of sprinkling range.

"This is highly unusual," he muttered nervously.

Please God, I prayed silently, don't let him lose his nerve now.

Mentally measuring the distance between himself and the mask-bearing wall, Padre Pedro shuffled forward on his dainty feet and unstopped the flask of Holy Water. Then he turned to me and said, "This won't harm the masks, will it?"

For a moment I had visions of the masks sizzling like scalded vampires at the Holy Water's sanctifying touch.

"No, Padre," I replied, "I don't think so. They've been treated many times with anti...anti..."

My mind had run suddenly into a stone wall and for some perverse reason all I could think to say was "anti-Christ". Obviously I was not about to tell Padre Pedro that my Devil Masks had been treated with anti-Christ, so instead I said, "Don't worry, Padre, Holy Water can't hurt them," which sounded just as bad, as if I were boasting of the masks' impermeable aura of evil.

Padre Pedro favored me with yet another anxious sidelong glance. All trace of pity was gone from his gaze now, replaced by what appeared to be undiluted fear. Then, taking a deep breath he edged a little closer to the wall and began to chant. The chanting went on far longer than it had on the two previous occasions. But finally, after what seemed like an eternity, the Padre raised the flask of Holy Water, stepped decisively forward, and sprinkled!

The Holy Water hit the masks just an instant after Padre Pedro's instep came down hard on Negra's tail, causing the offended feline to let out a piercing, blood-curdling scream. Startled nearly out of his senses, Padre Pedro lost his grip on the flask of Holy Water, which burst into a million pieces on the filthy tile floor.

When he had recovered his breath, the Padre crossed himself and walked quickly out of the house, with Rosa, her face convulsed with terror, close behind.

As they fled down the driveway they came within inches of crashing into Gerry, my octogenarian neighbor who, no doubt, was on his way over to borrow something he already owned six of himself.

"Hey," Gerry chuckled, jerking his thumb back over his arthritic shoulder, "who died?"

No Act Of Kindness

The moment I heard his voice I should have hung up the telephone. It was after all not a difficult voice to recognize: a deep, hoarse mechanical drone which rarely varied in volume or in tone, like a vacuum cleaner which someone has accidentally left running in the next room.

Ten years prior to that fateful call, Freddie had helped me to disengage myself from a somewhat touchy legal predicament. Fool that I was I still retained, all these years later, a smidgen of gratitude, which was why I did not do the sensible thing and hang up at once.

During the early months of my new life in Mexico I had found it almost impossible to distinguish between what was supposed to be legal and what was supposed to be illegal. One day my friend Nacho attempted to explain it to me.

"In Mexico," he said, "there is a law against almost everything, but everybody does whatever they want to anyway, even if sometimes you have to pay a mordida."

"A mordida?" I asked, "isn't that a bribe?"

"Well," he replied uncomfortably, "we prefer to think of it more like buying a permit—you know, after the fact."

Technically, at the time of the ill-fated favor, all of the foreign sales-people working in all of the resorts in Puerto Vallarta were required to obtain official working papers, called FM-3's. Naturally, the resort owners, working in close cooperation with the authorities, were able to find a way to drastically streamline this process, converting what should have been several filing cabinets full of forms into a single sheet of paper. This sheet contained a hand-written list of names, one of which was supposed to be my own. Due to the proverbial clerical error, however...

And so it was that I found myself in the parking lot of the *Vallarta Surf N Turf Vacation Club* with a uniformed gentleman on each arm inviting me, not to dance, but to be arrested and deported back to the United States of America for violating articles 33, 34, 35 and 36 of the Mexican constitution. As I was being led ignominiously away, into the breach leapt Freddie. Withdrawing from the front pocket of his permanent press polyester slacks a thick wad of bills, Freddie peeled off a C-note and promptly put a halt to the entire unpleasant proceedings. Had I only known then what being indebted to Freddie would entail, I would most likely have opted for deportation.

Freddie informed me over the phone that he was on his way to Palm Springs but was thinking of paying me a short visit first. "There's nothing I hate worse than waiting around in airports," he confided.

Because of that dangerous residue of gratitude and because his visit would necessarily be a brief one, I said, "Sure, come on over."

Freddie, devious bastard that he was, had neglected to mention two fairly significant details on the telephone. One of these became immediately apparent when he arrived at my house forty minutes later, not in a taxi, but in the business portion of an ambulance.

My long lost savior had always been grotesquely thin. But where lesser men might have chosen to disguise this fact, he went about with his shirt unbuttoned almost down to his waist, showing off to great disadvantage his concave chest as well as his twenty-four carat gold medallion. The medallion was roughly the size of Rhode Island and bore the image of a man teeing-off. It had been, according to Freddie, one of many first place trophies he had garnered during a brilliant collegiate golfing career.

"If it wasn't for my third serious car accident," he had confided to me on eleven or twelve occasions, "I could've turned pro."

I stood open-mouthed in my front yard as the driver and his assistant carried Freddie from the back of the ambulance on a stretcher. "Reinjured my back," he called out to me cheerfully. "Stupid bus drivers; you'd think they'd stop for a pedestrian once in a while."

"You got hit by a bus?" I croaked.

"Nah, he just winged me," Freddie said stoically. "Hey, tell these morons to put me on your terrace, will you."

The sight of Freddie being carried across my yard on a stretcher really should not have come as such a shock. He was not, as the saying goes, an accident waiting to happen; he was, in fact, a full-fledged catastrophe in progress.

An hour later Freddie let the other shoe fall. Lying on my prized chaise-lougne and facing the sparkling waters of Banderas Bay, with a vodka-toronja in one hand and a Marlboro Light in the other, he had begun to take on the frightening aspect of someone who was settling in.

"So, what time is your flight?" I asked as casually as I could manage.

"Flight?" he replied in his hoarse rumbling drone. "What flight?"

"Your flight to Palm Springs," I said nervously.

"Oh that flight," he said. "I gotta check my ticket, but I think it leaves in two weeks. Hey, how about a Percodan; my back's killing me."

Most visitors think of Puerto Vallarta as an ideal vacation spot with perfect weather, arm-fulls of charm and magnificent scenery. Most visitors, in the natural course of things, do not arrive during the rainy season.

It was late June when Freddie, like some giant polyester-skinned reptile, was deposited upon my terrace. From November until May this terrace is one of the most delightful spots on the Earth: a mere seventy meters from the ocean and favored with an optimum blend of sun, shade and breeze. But by late June the heat and humidity have climbed well above the comfort zone, the breeze has all but died and the summer fauna, consisting mostly of ants and mosquitoes, has all but taken over.

Freddie's arrival coincided precisely with the most unholy outbreak of ants I had ever seen. There were over twenty different species and they came in a shocking variety of colors and sizes: black, brown, reddish-brown, beige and quasi-transparent: huge, large, medium, small, mini and micro-mini.

The micro-minis, also known as humidity ants, materialized out of the thick summer air, were difficult to see individually with the naked eye and virtually impossible to eradicate.

The reddish-browns, also known as fire ants, came in a variety of sizes and were the most vicious, delivering painful stings wherever they came into contact with your skin. They were also impossible to exterminate, but unlike the humidity ants, could at least be put in their place now and then.

The largest ants were the leaf-cutters, capable of denuding an entire hibiscus bush in a matter of hours. These sneaky behemoths came out after dark, marching in long military columns from their nest to the target bush, and then back to their nest again carrying aloft pieces of leaf like trophies of war.

"Why don't you fumigate this dump?" Freddie asked me the next morning from his own nest atop the chaise-lounge.

"Say, Freddie," I said, "as far as your plans are…"

"I must look like a goddamn Chernobyl victim," he interrupted me. "I never got so many mosquito bites in my life. I still don't understand why I have to sleep outside. People treat their dogs better than this."

"I told you, Freddie, it's the cigarettes. Lucy can't stand the smoke. I mean, you're welcome to sleep inside, but then you'd have to crawl outside every fifteen minutes to poison yourself."

Freddie was either unable to walk, or else had convinced himself that he was unable to walk. Since his arrival he had slithered off of the chaise on only three occasions—to crawl to the bathroom and back.

"But your wife's not even here," he protested.

"I know," I replied feebly, "but the smell sort of lingers."

"Well, how long is she gone for?"

"Just a few days," I lied. Lucy had gone to California to visit her mother and was going to be away for almost a month.

"A few days?" Freddie said. "We better act fast."

"Act fast? What do you mean?"

"I mean, let's get a couple of whores over here pronto."

"Forget it!"

"Hey, I was just trying to make…"

"Ouch!" I yelled. Several red ants had climbed onto the terrace from the beach and were stinging my feet. I rushed inside to get the Raid.

"Hey, while you're up grab me another Percodan, will you," Freddie called after me.

By noon, the temperature/humidity index had passed the cruel and unusual mark, and Freddie was finally ready to reveal the ulterior motive for his visit.

He lay in his customary spot on the chaise while I sat at a small makeshift desk several meters away. Each of us had a pair of portable fans blasting into our faces from point-blank range, which made the summer heat almost bearable. Sweating continuously both night and day is conducive neither to comfort, nor good humor. And as I attempted to work on my long neglected novel, Freddie's droning interruptions ("Hey, check out the ass on *that* babe!") were pushing me dangerously close to the edge of violence.

"I have a confession to make," he said out of the blue.

"Oh, Christ," I moaned.

"You and I," he announced portentously, "are going to Orlando. Together."

"I don't think so," I replied. "And don't you mean, Palm Springs?"

"No. I lied about Palm Springs."

"You lied?"

"Yeah. I told you this was a confession."

"Well, if it's a confession, save it for the Padre. I don't want to hear it."

"Wait a minute," Freddie said. "Don't say anything. Just listen. I'm not asking for a *yes*. I just want you to keep an open mind. Fair enough?"

"Christ," I moaned again.

"You know," he droned on, "the mind is a lot like a parachute; if it's not open it doesn't work."

"Please, Freddie," I pleaded, "get to the goddamn point."

"So, you'll keep an open mind?" he persisted.

"Maybe you should be in the hospital, Freddie."

"Hey, my back's not *that* bad."

"I meant, a mental hospital."

"Very funny. Now, listen. I'm only going to lay this deal out for you one time."

"Thank God."

"This is the sweetest deal I've ever seen. You and me. Fifty-fifty. Two point over-ride. Housing. Seventy-five ups a day, guaranteed. Bonuses. Free passes to Disney World. Transportation. Unlimited…"

"Freddie, I've been out of the business for years. Haven't you heard?"

"Out of the business?" he repeated in tones of wonderment, as if I'd just announced that I'd grown a second penis.

"Yes."

"But, but, but what do you do for money?"

"My wife and I have a small gift shop," I replied.

"You mean, you're a shopkeeper?" Freddie said with disbelief.

"Yes."

"Hey, I'm sorry. No offense. But shopkeepers are losers. And I never thought of you as a loser."

"Thanks."

"Now, what I'm talking about is the chance of a lifetime. Just keep an open..."

One hour, ten cigarettes and two vodka-toronjas later, Freddie had laid out the entire "deal".

"I'm not interested," I said.

"You said you'd keep an open mind," he protested.

"No, I didn't."

"The resort's on a *golf course*, for Christ's sake!"

"I'm against golf," I said, just to irritate him. "It's ecologically unsound and elitist—a game for lazy rich people who want to pretend they're getting exercise. I mean, who ever heard of a sport where every player has a personal slave and you're not allowed to run?"

After a protracted and rather studied pause, Freddie said in an offended monotone, "I'm hurt. I mean, really hurt. Golf is a big part of my life. If it hadn't been for my third serious car accident, I could've been the next Tiger Woods. Which reminds me, the course in Orlando is designed by Jack Nicklaus and—hey, where are you going?"

"To the bathroom. I'm going to throw up."

"Probably that cheap bacon," Freddie advised me. "You should buy yourself some quality bacon for a change. Buying cheap bacon—it's all part of this cheap shopkeeper's mentality you've got yourself stuck in."

The ants had never been this bad before. The kitchen counter looked like a hallucination, there were so many micro-minis crawling all over it; the garden foliage was disappearing at a surreal rate, and my feet were so swollen with stings I could hardly put my shoes on. Apparently, it was time to rouse myself from the lethargy of low season and strike back.

Rosa, Chato and I gathered together on the terrace for a conference. Rosa, sweet, demure and highly paranoid, was our maid of many years. Chato, a short wiry man in his mid-fifties with the face of a career criminal, was our utterly dependable caretaker.

"Alright," I said, attempting to marshal the troops, "the ants are out of control. What are we going to do about it?"

Chato and Rosa regarded me with blank stares.

"The micro-minis," I suggested, "how do we stop them?"

"You'll never get rid of those little bastards," Chato stated. "But if you want to kill some just for the fun of it, there's a liquid poison you can inject into the beams with a hypodermic needle. Because that's where they have their nests, in the cracks in the beams."

"Fine," I said. "What about the fire ants?"

Rosa opined that they could not be killed either, but there was a way to keep them out. It consisted in "painting" a line with kerosene all around the house, forming an impenetrable perimeter, which Rosa claimed, the ants would not cross.

"Good," I said. "Now, how about the leaf-cutters? They're destroying the friggin foliage."

Chato, whose main responsibility was the garden, advised buying several kilos of powdered poison (it could be procured at the same store which sold the liquid variety). As soon as it got dark, he and I would follow the leaf-cutters back to their nest and pour the powder down the hole. This would not actually kill off the leaf-cutters, either, Chato explained. It would, however, force them to move to a new nest. After repeating the procedure enough times, they would locate their nest in someone else's yard, and it would then become their problem.

"Good," I told the troops, "let's get on this thing right…"

Suddenly I realized that I had lost their attention. Chato and Rosa were looking to my right and behind me at Freddie, who had chosen this moment to slither off of the chaise and begin crawling toward the bathroom. As they followed his slow painful progress, Rosa's eyes grew wide with suppressed terror. Chato's eyes clouded over with a cunning expression, which I recognized from the times I had observed him hunting iguanas with his slingshot.

"Excuse me," Rosa said timidly. "What is that man doing?"

"I think he's on his way to the bathroom," I said.

"But why doesn't he walk?" she asked.

"He hurt his back," I explained. "He was hit by a bus."

"And who is he talking to?" Chato wanted to know.

"No one," I said. "He just likes to talk, whether someone is listening or not."

"Is he a friend of yours?" Rosa asked.

"Not exactly. He did me a big favor one time, so I feel obligated to do one for him now. Let this be a lesson to the both of you."

"Is he staying long?" Rosa asked fearfully.

"I hope not."

Cutting short any further discussion, I dispatched Rosa and Chato to the far corners of Vallarta to purchase two gallons of kerosene, a paint brush, a kilo of powdered poison, a liter of liquid poison and a hypodermic needle. Hopefully they would not be stopped along the way by a curious policeman.

By the time they had left, Freddie had regained his perch atop the chaise. "What's for lunch?" he asked. Before I could answer, he said, "I'm out of insect repellant."

"There's more in the bathroom," I said.

"Great," he said with heavy sarcasm.

"Great what?" I asked.

"I was just in the bathroom," he said, giving me a meaningful look.

"How was it?" I asked.

"How was what?"

"The bathroom."

"You're enjoying this, aren't you?" Freddie demanded.

"Enjoying what?"

"My pain," he replied, wincing theatrically.

The truth was, I could not stand to see anyone in pain, which gave my houseguest a terribly unfair advantage. Slowly, I dragged myself out of my chair and headed into the house.

"Hey, while you're up, I could use another Percodan," he called after me.

When I returned with the repellant and the pain pill, Freddie could see from the strained look on my face that he'd perhaps gone too far. After knocking back the pill with several slugs of vodka-toronja and dowsing himself in enough repellant to *drown* a forest full of mosquitoes, he began to reminisce.

Remember so-and-so? Remember that time? Remember this time? Remember the good old days in general? Freddie's attempt to "re-bond" with me was so pathetically transparent that I ended up smiling, despite myself. This of course only encouraged him all the more.

"Hey, do you remember Ronnie O'Meara's motivational speech?" he asked.

"Which one?" I asked half-heartedly.

"The one about the ants," he said. "Pretty *apropos*, huh?"

"Oh, the ants. Right."

Freddie and I looked at each other, and as the details of that remarkable discourse came back to us bit by absurd bit, we broke into hysterical laughter.

Most of the sales managers I have known over the years have been what Mexicans call "special". Ronnie O'Meara was no exception.

A tall, oafish man, Ronnie had a head of wild, prematurely gray hair which grew in six or seven gravity-defying directions at once. He was manic to the point of being dangerous and everything he said made perfect sense, to him and him alone. Everyone assumed that Ronnie was on drugs; unfortunately for him, he was not.

Several weeks before his forced departure from Mexico, Ronnie delivered a truly memorable motivational speech to a roomful of bewildered sales people. Standing before us with his legs spread and a huge styrofoam cup of coffee in his hand, Ronnie stared hard at everyone for a full minute before announcing melodramatically:

"Ants don't sweat!"

Ronnie then took three enormous gulps of coffee, making his Adam's apple bounce up and down like a ping pong ball.

"The other day I was over at John and Mary's house," he finally went on.

John and Mary, most of us realized, were not real people, but rather an imaginary couple who played the role of the clients in Ronnie's favorite sales manual: *The Eye of the Tiger,* by Vick Vixby.

"And I saw," Ronnie said, striding back and forth, spilling coffee everywhere, "the most amazing thing." Ronnie paused for dramatic effect for what seemed like an hour, glaring at each of us in turn with the burning intensity of a medieval saint.

"But I'll tell you something," he finally said, lowering his voice to a conspiratorial whisper. "Most people wouldn't have thought it was so amazing. Most people, in fact, wouldn't even have seen what I saw."

"Not without a mouthful of mescaline," my neighbor mumbled.

"There in John and Mary's front yard," Ronnie rolled on, "was a small mountain. A miniature mountain about three feet high. That's strange, I thought to myself, I could've sworn that little mountain wasn't here a week ago, when I stopped by to return John and Mary the fifty dollars I had borrowed. What was even more strange was that the baby mountain was shaped exactly like a volcano. A volcano. Why, I could've been back on Maui."

Ronnie paused again to take another swallow of coffee and to stare up and off into space. We were all reasonably certain that he was supposed to be back on Maui, in what was left of his mind, staring up at a volcano.

"What's this?" I asked John and Mary. "What's this little volcano in your yard and how did it get there? 'Oh,' John and Mary said, 'that's just the ants.' Just the ants," Ronnie said, bemused. "Just the ants," he repeated matter of factly.

"Just the ants!" he thundered, waking up two closers in the back of the room.

Fortunately Ronnie's super-jumbo styrofoam cup was by now almost empty, because Ronnie always accompanied the raising of his voice with a violent gesture. As it was, he managed to spray the first row with brown drops and dislodge his shirttails from the tight confines of his black and white striped bermuda shorts.

With his white shirttails hanging out and over his ample gut Ronnie looked like a pregnant polar bear who has just stuck his paw into a light socket.

"So I began to observe," Ronnie said, quieting down again. "And what I observed were a whole lot of ants—thousands, maybe even millions of ants. And these ants, these tiny little creatures, what were they doing? I'll tell you what they were doing; each and every one of them was doing exactly the same thing. I know, because I sat there watching them for three hours."

Everyone knew that Ronnie was definitely making this part up. Short of receiving a massive blow to the head there was no way Ronnie could sit anywhere for three hours, let alone in a garden watching ants.

"On top of that miniature volcano," Ronnie rampaged on, "was a miniature crater—just like Haleakala back on Maui. And inside that crater was a teeny-weenie hole. And that hole was just like a two-lane tunnel I used to drive through when I was managing the Poconos Ski Club in Pennsylvania. One lane was for going inside the hole, and one lane was for going out of the hole. Entrance and exit. Egress and egret."

"I think an egret's a bird, Ron," Freddie, who was sitting in the back row, called out.

"Yeah, but what's an egress?" his buddy wanted to know.

Ronnie took advantage of this silly interruption to pour himself a full cup of coffee, causing everyone in the first three rows to visibly cringe.

"Now all of the ants," Ronnie roiled anew, "going into the hole were empty-handed. But every single ant exiting the hole was carrying a single grain of sand (which would be like me or you carrying a Volkswagen). And when the ant carrying the grain of sand reached the rim of the crater, he dropped it over the side. And down, down, down it tumbled, along the slope of the miniature mountain, making that miniature mountain just one grain of sand bigger." Long pause. Three gulps.

"Immediately," Ron resumed, "I mean absolutely at once, without even a second's hesitation, that ant turned around and went back into the hole to go get himself another grain of sand.

"And on and on it went. In and out. In and out. Grain by grain. Grain by grain. The mountain on the outside got bigger and taller; the ants' house on the inside got deeper and better. Because that's what those ants were doing— home improvement—making their common world a better place in which to live.

"And I'll tell you something. It was awful hot in John and Mary's front yard. But the ants never stopped to take a single break. Never complained. Never wished out-loud that they were someplace else, doing something different. They just kept on working, hour after hour, day after day, with nobody to pat them on the back. No one to offer them cash bonuses for exceeding their monthly goals. No one to give them special developer's discounts or bonus vacation incentives, or free trips for two to Mazatlan. No sir, those ants just kept doing their jobs, uttering nary a complaint, even though they knew in their heart of hearts that their job would never, ever be done."

Ronnie's pause had an air of finality this time. He stood there gulping from his eighteen-ounce styrofoam cup, soaked from head to toe despite the air-conditioning. Then he stood there some more, staring at us, and we sat there staring right back.

At that moment every person in the room was feeling exactly the same thing: a strong urge to pee, whether we had to or not. Just watching Ronnie drink all that coffee...

Finally, Trudy, one of our rookie sales people, someone so new to the business that she still suffered from the delusion that this was the kind of thing one was supposed to take seriously, raised her hand.

Ronnie inclined his dripping jungle of hair in her direction, gratitude written all over his face.

"I don't understand, Ron," Trudy said. "What's the point?"

Ronnie's head snapped back as if he'd received a physical blow.

"What's the point?" he repeated in amazement. "What's the point?"

"Yes," Trudy trudged intrepidly on, "what's the point? I don't get it."

"The point," Ronnie said ever so softly, "is quite simple. The point is something any child should be able to understand. The point is this: ANTS DON'T SWEAT!" he screamed.

Everyone in the front row ducked. But fortunately for all concerned, Ronnie had once again run out of coffee.

Over the course of the next several days, two separate battles were waged, but on widely different fronts. One campaign, Freddie's struggle to convince me to abandon everything of value in my life and run off with him to Orlando, met with but little success. The other, our war against the ants, produced what could only be described as mixed results.

Injecting poison into the wooden beams in the kitchen ceiling just seemed to make the micro-minis hungrier, while painting the Maginot Line around the entire outside of the house with kerosene did seem, at least at first, to produce encouraging results. The fire ants, repelled by the odor of the kerosene, did indeed seem reluctant to cross the line and almost at once my feet began to regain their normal shape.

Then it rained, one of those violent tropical deluges which washes every discarded plastic Clorox bottle from the rivers down into the bay, and it was as if the invincible line of kerosene had never existed. It had taken Chato three hours to encircle the house in the first place and I felt reluctant to have him do it all over again, especially when I knew that it would probably rain just as hard again the next day.

Our war against the leaf-cutters was more decisive. The first night Chato and I, accompanied by Freddie, who followed along behind us on all fours like a starving dog, discovered the nest with no difficulty and stuffed as much poison down it as we could. The next night, much to our satisfaction, we discovered that the ants had moved their nest about twenty meters across the yard. Once again we applied the poison, and sure enough the next night they had moved their beleaguered domicile once again, this time to the very edge of the property line. Two nights (and two more blitzkriegs) later, the leaf-cutters had had enough. In fact, I never saw a trace of them in my garden again, though shortly thereafter my neighbor's bougainvillea began mysteriously to disappear.

On the morning of the fifth day of my ordeal, as the sun rose majestically over the Sierra Madres, I was delighted to discover that Freddie's back had taken a turn for the better, and like the immediate predecessor to Cro-Magnon Man, he was now walking in a semi-erect position.

"Look's like the back's a lot better," I told him as he was leaving the bathroom.

"Yeah," he said cautiously, "I'm about half-way home now."

"Great," I said. "Pretty soon you'll be using tools."

After breakfast Freddie once again resumed his relentless droning.

"I hope you've finally made a decision," he told me as he doused himself with half a can of insect repellant.

"There was never any decision to make," I replied.

"So you're ready to come onboard?"

"I'm going to tell you this just one more time, Freddie. I'm not coming onboard. Frankly, I'd rather drown. I wish you luck in Palm Springs or Orlando, or wherever the hell you're going, and that's it."

"Is it the money?" Freddie asked. "Because, if it's the money, I think I can arrange a draw."

Instead of replying I sipped my coffee and looked out to the water where a small school of dolphins was swimming by.

"You know what I think the best thing would be," Freddie said, "is for you to try it out on a trial basis. No commitments. No strings. Say, a one-month trial basis. You don't like it, you say so; we'll shake hands and we'll still be friends."

"*Still* be friends?"

Freddie, who was immune to sarcasm, shame, irony and embarrassment of any kind, interpreted my last comment as a small ray of hope. "Yeah, we'll still be friends," he said with a faint, hoarse tinge of enthusiasm. "Even if, after a month of making more money than you ever made in your life, driving the nicest car you ever owned..."

"Freddie."

"Dating the most beautiful girls in Orlando..."

"Freddie."

"Even if, after all that success, you still decide to throw it all away so you can come back to this pitiful country to be a loser shopkeeper, I won't hold it against you. I'll still respect you. I'll still..."

"Freddie!"

"What?"

"Shut the fuck up!"

Unfortunately for Chato, the fire ants had renewed their siege of the terrace and I had no alternative but to send him downtown to buy another two gallons of kerosene.

Rosa, who was ordinarily reliable to a fault, had not shown up by noon and I began to worry. When Chato returned with the kerosene, I told him to just paint a quick line around the terrace—we'd leave the rest of the house for later. When he was done, he was to hop on the bus and go to Rosa's house to see what the problem was. The awful heat and humidity, the plague of ants and mosquitoes, even Freddie—I could survive all of these things if I had to. But no maid? Death was a more appealing alternative.

"That kerosene stinks," Freddie complained from the chaise. "It's ruining the taste of my vodka-toronja."

"You have a better idea?"

"Yeah, something modern, like DDT. You're living in the Stone Age here, for Christ's sake. Painting kerosene in the sand. Jesus! Maybe you should call in a witch doctor and get the place ex-communicated, while you're at it."

"Exorcised."

"Right. And another thing: I'd get rid of him," he said, pointing to Chato who was busily brushing kerosene onto the sand. "I don't trust him. He looks like he'd slit your throat in your sleep just to steal your shoes."

"He," I said severely, "is the most honest and trustworthy person I've ever known."

"You mean, he's the most honest *Mexican* you've ever known."

"No, Freddie, I mean person. Period."

"Ha, ha, ha," Freddie laughed. "You're trying to tell me that you'd trust him more than you'd trust...me, for example?"

"Let me put it this way, Freddie. If we had a list as long as the Manhattan phone book of all the people I knew in order of their trustworthiness, his name would be first, and yours would come right after Zyzynski."

"So you don't trust me?"

"I didn't say that."

"Is that why you won't come to Orlando? Because you don't trust me? Because you think I'll screw you once you help me set up the deal?"

"Trust has nothing to do with Orlando."

"Are you sure? Are you sure you aren't thinking: 'Hey, this guy needs me to pull this off, to get the ball rolling. But once the money's rolling in, once the developer's happy and the situation is solid, at that point, why should he want to split fifty-fifty with me? Why shouldn't he want all the money for himself?' That's what you're thinking, isn't it?"

"Actually, what I'm thinking, Freddie, is that you're the most obnoxious human being I've ever known."

"Hey," he said, taking a sip on his drink, "flattery will get you nowhere. But seriously, we've still got a deal, don't we?"

When Chato returned from his long bus ride, he reported to me that Rosa had not come to work because she was terrified of Freddie.

"That's ridiculous," I told Chato. "He may be weird, but he's basically harmless—unless you own a credit card."

"Oh, you know, Rosa's very superstitious," Chato said philosophically. "It's her Indian nature. You and I, we know he's just crazy. But to Rosa, mental illness is more like being possessed by a demon, or something."

Chato never ceased to amaze me. Though almost completely uneducated, he was cabable of remarkably sophisticated insights. "So you don't think she'll come back as long as Freddie's still here?" I asked him.

"I doubt it," he said. "Her sister told me she's already looking for another job."

Well, that was that.

Fortunately, my erstwhile roommate had never truly unpacked, so packing him back up again only took a few minutes. As he lay on the chaise smoking and drinking to the very last, I quickly finished stuffing his bags.

"I can't believe you're throwing me out," he said in his droning vacuum cleaner monotone.

"Nothing personal, Freddy," I said. "It's just a matter of priorities. Do I want an efficient and reliable maid, or do I want an annoying, chain-smoking, freeloading, pill-popping, vodka-swilling physically and emotionally crippled houseguest? No contest, really, if you stop to think about it."

"After all I've done for you," he said with disappointment, "it's hard to believe."

I laughed out loud.

"And it's because you're afraid of losing your maid?" he demanded with disbelief.

"Right."

"You actually value your maid more than you do my friendship?"

"Correct."

I had finished packing his bags and stood there wondering if I should wash my hands now or wait until after he had left. "So how do you want to go," I asked, "in another ambulance, or in a plain old taxi?"

Freddie opted for a taxi, which was soon arranged. The driver and I helped Freddie get his many bags into the trunk, while Freddie stood there complaining the whole time about my lack of gratitude and my shabby notion of "true-friendship". Even as he climbed into the backseat, he would not let it alone.

"I still can't believe it," he said.

"What?"

"That a man who I saved from prison and God knows what else, could treat me like some old newspapers you just throw out with the garbage. I guess my father was right after all. No act of kindness, he used to tell me, goes unpunished."

Nacho Knows Best

Nacho, despite the fact that he had once caused me to run over my gardener, was someone whose friendship I had always valued. Over the years he had bombarded me with such a colossal amount of unsolicited and largely useless advice that on more than one occasion I had felt the overpowering urge to take out a gun and shoot him.

But Nacho was *always* absolutely certain of his facts. No matter how arcane or how trivial the question, Nacho possessed the definitive answer. When, on those rare occasions (due to some extraordinary breach in the very fabric of Cosmic Continuity) Nacho did *not* know where you should go or what you should do, a sort of volitional vacuum was created in which your only apparent option was to stay at home and do nothing.

In retrospect, staying at home and doing nothing would have been by far my best move when Nacho suggested that I take my annual two-week retreat at the Netzahualcoyotl Hot Springs.

"Netza...say, what?"

"Netzahualcoyotl," Nacho began in his maddeningly precise and pedantic way, "was one of the minor Aztec emperors whose power reached its zenith shortly before the conquest. Today, he is best remembered as a great promoter of the arts, as well as a talented poet in his own right. The most famous of his poems, many of which were preserved by Father Francisco De La Cruz…"

"Nacho," I said, interrupting my friend, "I have a pressing engagement early next week. Could we stick to the Hot Springs, please?"

"The Netzahualcoyotl Hot Springs," Nacho changed gears with no apparent effort, "are located high up on the eastern flank of the Nevada de Toluca Volcano in the state of Mexico, which should not be confused with…"

"I know where the volcano is, Nacho."

"The Hot Springs sit at an elevation of approximately four thousand one hundred and twenty-two meters, which in feet…"

Nacho had on more than one occasion actually talked me to sleep, a fate I will attempt to spare the reader by summarizing the remainder of his discourse, which crawled on for so long we had made the transition to Daylight Savings by the time he was finished.

The Netzahualcoyotl Hot Springs were extremely isolated, rarely frequented and located in a wild and beautiful setting. Set by the side of a rushing river, the sprawling complex contained two pools, a small rustic hotel and an equally rustic restaurant serving fresh trout. Winding as it rose gradually from the end of the property was an old abandoned logging road, along which one could walk all the way up to the cone of the volcano.

It sounded ideal, especially for my purposes. After a stress-filled year of responding to the same two touristic inquiries over and over again ("What's with all the skeletons?" and "Do you like living here?"), I was in desperate need of a break. A peaceful, unpeopled place where I could take infinitely long and solitary walks, bathe in thermal waters and attempt to unsnarl the matted ending of my novel was almost too good to be true.

The moribund bus dropped me off near the end of the road, then turned on its wobbly wheels to begin the suicidal plunge back down the mountainside. I found myself standing at the foot of a heavily traveled goat-trail, surrounded by steep pine covered ridges and spectacular gorges. It was a wild and savage country, bathed in swirling mists and a fine ceaseless rain. Totally alone, I felt the mood of the immense mountain overwhelming me.

From where I stood the Hot Springs entrance was only two hundred yards away. I set off at once, suffused with optimism and a sense of boundless, timeless wonder.

My sojourn into the land of Samadi lasted nearly an entire minute, or the time it took me to walk twenty paces up the steep trail. Too late, I recalled Nacho's warning (lost among a million others) not to exert myself on my first day at an elevation of 13,396 feet.

All at once I was on my knees gasping for breath, my heart smashing murderously against the narrow walls of my oxygen-challenged chest. Putting my timeless mood for the moment on hold, I waited to die.

But of course I didn't die. Little by little, crouching on my hands and knees and panting like a bedraggled dog who has just had his way with all the bitches in the neighborhood, I began to recover.

After a while a couple of campesinos came walking by leading a pair of skinny burros. The two men stopped and stared at me uncertainly.

"What are you doing?" one of them asked me.

Rising unsteadily to my feet I told them between gasps that I was having a heart attack. "Perhaps," I added, "you could give me a ride up to the springs. I'll be happy to pay you fifty pesos."

The men insisted on payment up-front—just in case I expired along the way. Then they dumped the pile of firewood off one of the burro's backs and loaded me on in its place. Ten minutes later I made my triumphant entrance through the gates of the Netzahualcoyotl Hot Springs, sliding off the skinny rear end of a malnourished ass.

The NHS was nestled in a narrow mist-shrouded valley and consisted of a large compound dotted with pools of boiling water and a half dozen rustic structures, the largest of which was the "hotel". Nacho had described the NHS as "rarely frequented", which was not exactly how I found it. I found it full of four hundred frenetically squealing thirteen year old girls on a field trip from their school in Toluca, an excursion which had apparently been timed to coincide with the precise moment they all reached puberty.

After several panicked inquiries, I discovered that the kids would be leaving in a few hours, so I decided to go for a very slow walk up that wonderful gradually sloping logging road so painstakingly described to me by Nacho. Finding the road was not difficult: it was merely a continuation of the interrupted road up to the Hot Springs. Setting foot on it was another matter. The road was blocked by a locked gate and guarded by an unfriendly looking fellow holding a shotgun.

"The road is closed," he said.

"Closed?"

"Yes," he said. "They're dynamiting. No one can go up there until they're finished."

"When will that be?" I asked.

"Quien sabe?" he said helpfully.

"Well, how long has the work been underway?" I asked.

"About five years."

It was then that I recalled Nacho mentioning in passing that he had last visited the Netzahualcoyotl Hot Springs over twenty years ago. This was the principle pitfall in attempting to base one's actions on Nacho's helpful information: there was so much of it, small but key pieces tended to get lost in the shuffle, like mismatched socks in a laundromat.

Though the NHS, as well as the road, ran through a narrow valley with steep impenetrable terrain surrounding it on both sides, there was, I discovered, a long meadow which paralleled the road, rising gradually into the distance. Determined to walk somewhere, I climbed a barbed wire fence in order to explore this pastoral piece of terrain, and to kill time until the kids had left.

Unfortunately, this was an area of almost continuous precipitation and the meadow, once I actually set foot on it, proved to be a bit on the boggy side. Nonetheless, I trudged intrepidly upriver, sinking up to my ankles in mud, until I came to another barbed wire fence. And then another. And then another. And then, I gave up.

Back at the Netzahualcoyotl Hot Springs, the children had all departed in a flotilla of ancient yellow buses, and now at least the place was blissfully deserted. It was also getting rather late so I decided to reserve my room. The door to the hotel was locked, naturally, and there was no bell. Not knowing what else to do, I proceeded to bang on the door and yell at the top of my voice, "Buenas tardes!" over and over again. Five minutes of this noisemaking got me absolutely nowhere, so I went to go look for a human being.

Thirty yards upriver from the hotel was a much smaller building with a sign falling off of it which read, "Office". Inside, I found a pair of men, one old and fat, the other young and thin, sitting at a small table playing dominos.

"I'd like a room," I told them.

"It's a hundred pesos a night for nationals," the fat one, who turned out to be the manager, told me, "and five-hundred pesos for foreigners."

When I handed the man a hundred pesos, he said that I would have to pay another four hundred because, obviously, I was a foreigner.

"But I live in Mexico," I protested.

"You can live anywhere you want to," he said, laying down a double-three, "you're still a foreigner."

"That's absurd," I said. "Not to mention illegal. Let me speak to your superior."

His superior, it turned out, was in the "main office" in Toluca, several hours away. "Well, let's call him," I said.

The marvels of telephonic communication had not yet reached the Netzahualcoyotl Hot Springs, so picking up the microphone of a rusty two-way radio, the manager called his boss.

"There's a foreigner here," he shouted into the microphone, "who claims to be a Mexican and wants to pay the national rate. Over."

"Absolutely not," a voice crackled out of the radio. "Over."

"Sorry," the manager said, "he says absolutely not."

"I heard him," I said. "May I speak with him myself, please?"

The manager reluctantly handed me the microphone and the following conversation ensued.

"I may be a foreigner," I said, "but I have lived in Mexico for many years, so I am not a tourist."

For ten seconds I stood there like a fool, waiting in vain for a reply.

"Say 'over,'" the manager advised me.

"Over," I said with disgust.

"You live in Mexico City?" the man in the radio asked accusingly. "Over."

"No, I live in Puerto Vallarta. Over."

"You're a long way from Puerto Vallarta. Over."

"I am aware of that. Over."

"But you are not a tourist? Over."

"No, I am not a tourist. Over."

"Then what are you doing at the Netzahualcoyotl Hot Springs? Over."

"I'm doing research for the Mexican Tourist Bureau, for whom I work," I lied. "Over."

"What kind of research? Over."

"I'm investigating discriminatory pricing practices at remote touristic destinations. Over."

"Oh…Over."

"So what's my room number?" I asked the manager, who had returned to his dominos game.

"They'll tell you over there," he said.

"Over where?"

"At the hotel."

"There's nobody at the hotel. That's why I came over here."

"Are you sure?"

"Positive."

"Well," he said, laying down a six-two, "someone will be over there soon."

"How soon?"

"It's hard to say."

"Is the restaurant open?" I asked.

"Of course. Why wouldn't it be?"

The restaurant, a small log cabin which looked as if it had almost survived a mudslide, was indeed open. The décor was Neo-Neanderthal. Instead of chairs there were termite ridden tree trunks. The tables were slabs of rough wood, some with the bark still on them. I chose one of the barkless tables and sat down.

The waiter, who also quadrupled as the cook, cashier and dishwasher, took my order without enthusiasm and thirty minutes later I was served what appeared to be a pan-fried guppy.

For a moment I sat there staring at his tiny tail and wondering what had happened to his parents.

"This could qualify as child-abuse," I told the waiter.

"No, no. It's absolutely fresh," he assured me.

The poor little fish was accompanied by a badly wrinkled baked potato and a mound of non-specific greenish flora. The trout, truly the smallest I had ever seen, I consumed in one swallow. The green matter and the potato, which you could tell had been grown underground, I left alone, despite the fact that I was faint from hunger.

"Do you have any bread?" I asked the waiter, hoping to fill myself up on something.

"No," he said with condescension, "we only serve tortillas."

"Great, I love tortillas."

"So do I," the waiter said. "Too bad we don't have any."

"What about rice? Have you got any rice?"

"We did," the waiter said, "six kilos. But the rats got it."

"Alright," I moaned, "bring me five more trout."

An hour later, still famished, I returned to the hotel, which was still locked, and began pounding on the door again. After several minutes the skinny young man who had been playing dominos unlocked it from the other side and let me in.

"What do you want?" he asked.

Summoning vast reserves of self-control, I replied, "My room."

Yawning and vigorously scratching at his left ear, he said, "You have number five."

"And the key?" I asked, gritting my teeth.

"The key is kind of hard to get to," he said.

The key, all the keys in fact, were hanging on nails at the back of a small alcove. The door to the alcove was locked and, according to the young man, could not be opened because the key to it had been lost for almost a year. In order to reach the room keys one had to scramble over a narrow chest-high counter, which needless to say, I was not about to do.

"What's your name?" I asked him.

"Nacho," he said.

Briefly, I wondered if murdering two people named Nacho would get me into the *Guinness Book of Records*.

"Well, Nacho," I said, "if I'm not mistaken, you work here. Am I right?"

"Yes," Nacho said. "I have worked here ever since I was a child."

"And what exactly is your job?"

"I'm the assistant manager," he said proudly.

"And who else works here? At the hotel, I mean."

"Just me," he said bitterly. "No one helps me. I have to do everything."

"Well," I said reasonably, "since you do everything, how about climbing over the counter. And getting me my goddamn key!"

Watching Nacho maneuver himself awkwardly over the high counter was, up to that point, the highlight of my entire day. When he handed me the key, it was attached to a small log with the number five scrawled on it in fluorescent orange paint.

"Thank you," I said.

Nacho said, "You're welcome," and then disappeared.

Leading off of the small circular lobby was a long, dark narrow corridor with doors running along both sides. Halfway down the left side I found number five. Naturally, the lock was oxidized. Badly bruising my knuckles on the absurd little log, I struggled forever to get it open. Finally, the blasted thing gave. I opened the door and stepped inside.

The damp dim windowless room appeared to have been transferred intact from the set of *Schindler's List*. Roughly the size of a mini-van, it contained two incredibly narrow bunk beds, another tree stump and a lamp with no bulb. Just for laughs, I picked up the small pillow from the bottom bunk. It was shaped like a football and felt lumpy to the touch, as if it had been filled with clumps of dirt.

It was getting dark now and the temperature was dropping rapidly. Removing two sweaters and a coat from my pack, I put them on and extracted my writing tablet and a couple of pens. The hotel, as far as I could tell, was totally deserted. At least I would get some writing done in peace—if I didn't freeze or starve to death first.

Back in the small lobby once again, I eyed the handful of badly battered chairs set around the large empty fireplace. A fire would have made the place nice and cozy, I thought, and when several moments later Nacho returned, I asked him about the possibility of getting one going.

"Well, yes, a fire would be nice," he replied, "but unfortunately I forgot to bring in the wood and now it's too wet." Then he disappeared again.

It was quite dark now so I turned on all of the lights and sat down to do some work. After several hours I was beginning to make some serious progress on the tangled ending of my novel. Then Nacho returned.

"Oh," he said, "I see that you are writing."

"Very observant," I muttered, without looking up.

"Yes, I have always had excellent vision."

"Congratulations," I said.

"Did you like the trout?" he asked.

"Yes," I said, adding in English, "you chicken-brained moron."

"I caught them myself," Nacho said proudly.

"With your bare hands?"

"No, I used a rod and reel—a gift from an appreciative guest," he said suggestively. "I understand you ate six entire trout. You must have been hungry."

"I'm still hungry."

"Oh," Nacho said. "Unfortunately, the kitchen is closed."

"Naturally."

`For several minutes Nacho stood in the center of the room staring guiltily at the empty fireplace, while I stared at my writing tablet, praying he'd disappear again.

"I hope the high altitude here is not affecting you adversely," Nacho said, just as I was beginning to regain my lost train of thought.

"No," I said, "but the damp freezing air is giving me a sinus headache."

"Well, in that case," Nacho suggested, "you should drink the juice of several limes. Limes contain a great deal of vitamin C."

"Really? Do you have any limes?"

"No."

I picked up my pen and began to write again.

"The altitude here affects many of our visitors who are not used to it," Nacho said. "We are at an elevation of four thousand, one hundred and twenty two meters, which in feet would be…"

"Wait a minute!" I said, dropping my pen. For the first time I took a good long look at him. There was something eerily familiar about his face.

"You know," Nacho said, "I'm afraid I must apologize for the lack of amenities here. I have tried to improve things, but no one listens to my suggestions. For example, in my opinion, the hotel should have been built closer to the pools. As it is, our guests must walk a total of seventy-five meters from the hotel to the pools, and then another seventy-five meters from the pools back to the hotel. To me, this seems an excessive amount of distance. What is your opinion?"

"So what was your suggestion, Nacho, that they move the hotel, or that they move the pools?"

"Also," Nacho said, ignoring my question, "there is an important lack of cultural background available to the guests. Did you know, for example, why the Netzahualcoyotl Hot Springs are called the Netzahualcoyotl Hot Springs?"

"Yes."

"Well then," Nacho said, "you are one of the lucky few. Towels are another of our shortcomings. In my opinion, our towels are rather small. In fact, they measure only…"

"Excuse me, Nacho," I said, repressing the urge to take my pen and drive it through his heart. "How old are you?"

"I am twenty-one years old. I was born on November 20, which you may not realize, since you are a foreigner, is an important date in Mexican history. On that date one-hundred and…"

"And you were born where?"

"I was born right here at the Netzahualcoyotl Hot Springs. My mother was the maid at the time and…"

"And your father?" I asked.

"Unfortunately, he died before I was born. That is why I was never able to get to know him personally."

"That's too bad," I said consolingly. "If he was already dead, I can see how getting to know him personally would have been difficult."

"Yes, but my mother gave me his name," Nacho said. "In honor of his memory. I will be honest with you. I am very unhappy here. One day I may have to resign my position. It's all the manager's fault. He has very poor judgement. For example, when you checked in, I feel he should have informed you of the fact that tomorrow we are expecting a large group; one of the largest we have ever had. I am afraid that all of the rooms have been booked, so you will have to leave. Check out time is officially nine A.M., but I am certain that if you wish to stay until ten, or even ten-thirty, that will not present a problem."

"What?"

"Tomorrow, we are expecting a large group; one of the largest we have ever had. I am afraid…"

"Nacho?"

"Yes?"

"Shut up."

I made it back to Vallarta late the following afternoon. The first thing I did upon my arrival was to call my friend, the other Nacho.

"Back so soon?" he said. "What happened?"

"It's a long story. By the way, Nacho, were you by any chance at the Netzahualcoyotl Hot Springs around the twentieth of February in 1978?"

There was a long silence on the line while Nacho did some mental arithmetic. "Yes," he said finally, "how in the world did you know that?"

"Nacho," I said, grinning maliciously into the mouthpiece, "are you sitting down?"

Jumping To Delusions

At a certain point in life one either becomes a good deal calmer, or else grows increasingly nervous. Somehow, and for reasons even my Past-Lives Therapist was at a loss to explain, my lamentable lot had been cast with the neurotics—the chronically anxious, the incurably apprehensive.

All day long I'd been skating fitfully along the jagged edges of an all-out Level Six anxiety attack. When I arrived home, my wife, normally a calming influence, managed to nudge me right off the charts with three matter-of-factly spoken words:

"The bank called."

"What bank?" I inquired breathlessly.

The night before I had committed a grave error; I had watched the movie *Alien 12*. And as the tentacles of panic began to slip through the chinks in my woefully inadequate psychic armor, I was reminded most unpleasantly of the scene in which the hideously revolting, mucous-dripping, multi-limbed monster slithers its slimy way simultaneously into seven separate human orifices, leaving the young and largely nude female victim…well, upset to say the least.

"*Your* bank," my wife replied, her attention already drifting back to *Vanity Fair*.

"You mean, *Banco Sinfondos*?"

"Yes," she said. "Someone named Garcia, or Gonzales, or Godzilla; I can't remember."

"Well, w-what did he want?"

"How should I know?"

"But what did he say?"

"He said you should come to the bank tomorrow before three. And be sure to bring your passport."

My *passport*? Like a demented computer my mind began to sift with lightning speed through all of the awful possibilities: bounced checks, insufficient funds, misplaced funds, internal audits, external audits, deportation, institutionalized torture, court-ordered castration. The fact that I had, to the best of my knowledge, done nothing even remotely unsavory counted for naught, as that curious phenomenon known as "Expatriate Paranoia" took over the rational centers of my forebrain and reduced them to frontal egg foo-yung.

That night I slept little, only long enough to have a terrifying dream in which I was being chased across a stark desert landscape by a uniformed Chipotle Chile wearing a "Young Republicans" baseball cap and riding astride a fire-breathing burro.

The next day, passport in hand, I walked trembling into the downtown branch of Banco Sinfondos and asked for Sr. Garcia, or Sr. Gonzales. I was fairly certain that if in fact there was a Sr. Godzilla working in a bank in Puerto Vallarta, then he would be connected with *Sumitomo*, and not *Sinfondos*.

"Sr. Garcia just stepped out," a polite woman in "Customer Service" informed me. "Is there any way that I can help you?"

Yes, if you work nights as a bail bondsman, I thought.

"Yes," I said aloud. "Sr. Garcia called my home yesterday and requested my presence here at the bank. I was just wondering what it was about."

"I am awfully sorry," the nice woman said, "but I have no idea."

"He asked me to bring my passport with me," I added.

"He did?" she said, surprised. "Well, he may be back just before closing. You might try returning then."

I did not return to the bank just before closing. Instead I went home and downed three quick shots of Raicilla, chasing that clarified snake venom with a quarter cup of Melox Plus. Feeling somewhat calmer, I then began to pace nervously back and forth across the living room, analyzing my options: joining the French Foreign Legion, suicide, moving to Yelapa...

"Honey, I'm home!"

It was my wife, returning home after a fun-filled afternoon of purging *Sam's Club* of the majority of its contents.

When I did not respond immediately to her greeting, she yelled, "Help!"

This meant that I should race outside and help her to unburden her vehicle, which groaned audibly with pleasure as I removed from its interior the twenty gallon drum of Clorox, the one hundred pound bag of cat food and the largest jar of mayonnaise known to humankind.

"What's with the mayonnaise?" I asked my wife. "Are we opening a torta stand? Are we having the entire state of Jalisco over for tuna salad sandwiches?"

"Very funny. The bank called again," she replied striding past me.

"What? When? What'd they say?"

"Just a minute."

Before responding to my crucial query, she first found it necessary to visit the ladies room, pour herself a mineral water and then make three urgent phone calls. I managed, with difficulty, to make it halfway through the second call.

"What did they want?" I shouted.

"I'll call you back in five minutes," my wife told her manicurist.

After she had hung up, she favored me with a certain look, one she normally reserved for our dog when he threw up on something inappropriate.

"It was a Sr. Garcia calling," she said, "I wrote it down this time."

"Yes, yes," I said impatiently, "I know his name."

"He said you won a prize, some kind of special drawing they have, and if you don't claim it before three tomorrow, you lose it."

A prize?

In order to catch parole violators in the United States, the police would on occasion call these individuals up and tell them that they had won something and could they come to such and such a place at such and such a time, and so on. Naturally, when they showed up to claim their prizes, they were arrested. Could this be what was happening to me? No, I decided, that would be far too complicated. And then I suddenly remembered having seen posters all over the bank with pictures of brand new cars on them.

"I've won a car!" I screamed.

"A car? my wife said. "How do you know?"

"They had posters of cars all over the bank. I didn't read them of course, but that has to be it. I think it was a Chrysler. Or a Ford."

The next day, having spent another restless night, I was at the bank before ten. Sr. Garcia was in and already seated behind a large desk in a small partitioned cubicle. When I introduced myself, he seemed enormously pleased to see me. "Congratulations!" he said, warmly shaking my hand.

"Gracias. Gracias," I said. "I can't believe it. I've never won anything in my life."

"Well, you're a winner now," Sr. Garcia beamed. "Please, have a seat. We have a number of forms to fill out."

"Yes, I can imagine," I said.

"Did you bring your passport?" he asked.

"Of course."

"We have to be quite certain of your identity, as you must realize, when giving away such a valuable prize."

"Yes, yes, I understand."

As it turned out, there were an absurd number of forms to be filled out and signed, and the process was further delayed by Sr. Garcia's disappointment with the quality of my signatures.

"You have signed your name ten times here," Sr. Garcia said a tad sternly, "and no two signatures are exactly alike."

"I'm sorry," I said. "I guess I'm a little excited."

"I understand," Sr. Garcia said kindly. "Here, let's just see if you can make all the signatures look like this one." He presented for my inspection the card I had signed when first opening my account, and I assiduously attempted to make all ten of my required new signatures more or less match the old one.

"Not bad," Sr. Garcia said. "They're not an exact match, but I think they're close enough. It might not be a bad idea, however, to sit down and practice a little when you have some spare time."

There is no telling what I might have replied to this bizarre suggestion under normal circumstances. Things being what they were, I simply said, "Of course." At that point I would have agreed to sawing my mother in half, if it meant I would finally get my hands on the keys.

"Alright," Sr. Garcia said portentously, "I'll be right back."

Right back with the pink slip, I thought, fairly certain he was not about to drive the car into his cubicle.

Ten agonizing minutes later Sr. Garcia returned with a cardboard box, laying it ceremoniously atop his desk. "Well, there it is!" he said triumphantly. "Congratulations!"

There were many words printed on the various sides of the box, but by far the two largest were: "Sandwich Maker".

"What's this?" I asked, dumbfounded.

"It's an electric sandwich maker," Sr. Garcia announced with pride.

"A what?"

"It's really quite marvelous. Among its many features are," he went on, reading off the box, "a 'non-stick cooking surface', a 'cool touch housing and handle', a 'power light' (which tells you when it's on), and a 'ready light' (which tells you when it's ready). And as you can see, it also 'crimps and seals sandwiches in half'. Quite an apparatus," he concluded.

"But, what about the car?"

"What car?" Sr. Garcia asked.

"The one on all the posters."

"Oh, that's our annual prize. You've won the monthly prize."

"So this is it?" I said. "A *sandwich maker*?"

"That's correct," Sr. Garcia said. "Once again, on behalf of Banco Sinfondos, congratulations!"

"Thanks," I said. "Although, all things considered, I think I would've preferred being deported."

Feet First

I am often asked by my clients if travelling all over the interior of Mexico, which my wife and I do almost every summer, is dangerous. Usually, I reply in the negative, explaining that while we may be adventurous, we are not suicidal. Left unsaid is the fact that it can be dangerous, but in subtle ways I prefer not to explain; my time, I have found, is better spent explaining to these clients why, before leaving my shop, they should spend as much of their money as possible.

The quaint colonial town of Taxco is a perfect example of the less obvious dangers of travel in Mexico. Though the odds of being mugged there are almost nil, a number of other equally frightening possibilities await the unsuspecting traveler.

Purely by chance, we happened to arrive in Taxco just in time for the town's annual Saint's Day. Night was quickly falling and the small main square had already gone into fiesta-overdrive. Packed solid with festive humanity, the square was all done up in colored lights, strings of pica-papel, balloons and banners. The popcorn, peanut and hot dog vendors were scooping, salting and frying for all they were worth and one of those charming off-key brass bands was playing its heart out inside the zocalo.

Facing the square and dominating it entirely was the Church of Santa Prisca, one of the most lovely in all Mexico.

The church and its small forecourt were surrounded by a tall iron fence. It was against this fence that Lucy and I had decided to lean while we polished off our corn-on-the-cobs and waited for the fireworks to start.

Our corns, as is the custom, had been liberally slathered with mayonnaise, grated cheese and chile powder. By the time I had finished mine, my moustache was a goopy mess. After a pathetic attempt to wipe it off with my tiny useless napkin, I made the mistake of asking my wife how I looked. "Fine," she said. "Except your moustache looks like it's covered with white, blood- flecked snot."

The highlight of the evening's festivities, according to the corn vendor, was to be a uniquely Mexican demonstration of pyrotechnic mayhem known as "The Burning of the Torritos". Neither of us had actually seen a torrito being burned before, but we had the impression that it was supposed to be colorful and fun for the whole family.

"Here it comes! Here it comes!" a voice shouted.

From out of the densely packed crowd, a man appeared carrying the odd and cumbersome looking contraption balanced on his shoulders. The torrito consisted of a paper-mache bull mounted on a bamboo frame with all manner of odd little objects attached to it. The torrito man, now the center of attention, lit a cigarette and touched its glowing tip to one of those odd little do-dads. There was a short pregnant pause...and then...rockets, sparks, firecrackers and other bits of explosive debris began to fly from the torrito in all directions, as the man who held it took off like a rocket himself, charging into the crowd horns first with the apparent intention of doing serious bodily harm to anyone unfortunate enough to cross his path.

"Well, this is kind of intense," I told my wife, as the festive crowd surged joyfully around us and small rockets flew whistling by our ears.

"Do you think it's dangerous?" Lucy asked.

"I don't think so," I said, scanning the crowd. "No one looks very worried."

"*Right*," Lucy said.

What my wife meant was that Mexicans and Americans have, as a rule, somewhat different notions as to what the word "dangerous" means; and that fear of bodily injury is not necessarily taken with the same degree of gravity "down South" as it is in more northern climes.

"Don't be such a gringa..." I began to chide my wife, when three more torritos were suddenly lit and sent rushing into the crowd of revelers, whose only reaction was to cheer and clap their hands. With four of these infernal devices now circulating inside a fairly confined space, the air was quickly filling with smoke and it was becoming difficult to see, as well as breathe.

Then, out of the gloom, there loomed a fifth torrito. In the next instant it became apparent that the psychotic individual toting this latest exquisitely handcrafted engine of destruction was heading unmistakably in our direction. With our backs scrunched up against the iron fence, our options, escape-wise, were severely limited. Sidling as best we could desperately to our left, we succeeded in bowling over a short young man and stepping on the toes of *two* pregnant women. Meanwhile, rockets continued to whiz past our heads, firecrackers to explode at our feet and large colorful sparks to embed themselves in our hair and clothing. My wife, with the finely honed survival skills of a typical North American Female, found the open gate to the churchyard (the only place in the small square off-limits to the demented torrito-men) and ducked nimbly inside.

Instead of following immediately in Lucy's prudent footsteps, I paused to help the young man, who I had capsized, to regain his feet. The poor fellow had been so determined not to drop an object which he held desperately to his breast that he had neglected to cushion his fall with his hands. And so, he'd gone down hard, landing squarely and painfully on his coccyx.

For almost an entire second, I felt an unpleasant wave of First-World guilt washing over me. Big blundering gringo that I was, I had simply bowled this small Third-World individual over, and in his own backyard, no less. But was it my fault, I wondered, transmuting at once my guilt into anger, that this sawed-off idiot was too stupid to cover his own buttocks? Then my eyes alit upon the small stone sculpture he held so tightly in his hands and I understood at once the man's willingness to suffer a badly bruised backside.

It was exquisite—the carving, not his rear-end. Roughly eight inches high and four wide, it was done in a black, opaque stone and represented an Aztec Eagle Warrior embracing his Eagle Spirit.

"How beautiful!" I said.

The young man's dark intense eyes, which had been glaring at me with naked hostility, suddenly lit up like a pair of Christmas trees. "You like it?" he said eagerly.

"Yes, very much," I replied. "Are you the artist?"

"Yes. My name is Vicente Hidalgo Calderon, and my work is for sale," he said with a charming blend of dignity and greed.

Vaguely, over my shoulder, I could hear Lucy calling out my name along with urgent instructions to get myself the hell out of there. Another two torritos had been fired-up and there was really no safe place left in the entire square: seven madmen, exploding bulls atop their shoulders were now charging repeatedly into the crowd, scattering widows, nuns and orphans indiscriminately in their wake.

But Vicente and I continued to stand with our backs to the iron bars, oblivious, or nearly so, to the carnage going on all around us. There and then I asked him the price of his sculpture, which he refused to give me. Instead, he invited me to visit him the following day at his home where he could show me more of his work and we could discuss the entire matter "con calma". I quickly agreed. He gave me his card. We shook hands and said good-bye.

It was only then that I thought to look for my wife. I found her a few moments later in the churchyard, crouching in the leeward shadow of an immensely fat taco vendor. "Next best thing to a bomb shelter," she said, smiling up at me.

The following morning we set out to find Vicente's house which was located in the Colonia Santa Marta, a poor neighborhood on the outskirts of town.

Leaving the Hotel Buena Vista was always a problem for me, due to the unusual and unnatural relationship I had developed with Sr. Brussell, the manager. Sr. Brussell was a middle-aged Englishman who possessed several unfortunate qualities: an awful knack for hideously disfiguring the Spanish language; and an equally disquieting lack of command of his large intestine—his thunderous attacks of flatulence had actually woken me from a sound sleep the previous night. Behind his back, Lucy and I had taken to calling him, Sr. Brussell Sprout.

In order to avoid Sr. Brussell, who was constantly on the prowl for me, we had to sneak out of the hotel via the steep back stairs. In Taxco, which is built on the side of a mountain, everything is steep, and narrow. Once we had crept, like a pair of burglars, down the steep narrow stairs, we found ourselves on the steep narrow street. Our next order of business was to flag down a taxi. But to do that we had to travel to the nearest plaza, one of the many small flat-spots which dotted the town like base camps on the side of Mt. Everest. The plaza was only two blocks away, but given the difficulty of getting around Taxco on foot, it seemed considerably further.

As we began to shuffle down the acute cobble-stoned incline, hugging the walls of buildings, which lined both sides of the canyon-like street, I wondered what one was supposed to do when a car passed. There were no sidewalks and the street was just wide enough to accommodate a single vehicle.

"I hear a car," Lucy said.

There were, in fact, three cars and as they rounded the curve above us, we froze, like deer caught in the glare of oncoming headlights. The cars were traveling at unwholesome speeds, and we had only a moment to react. But react we did, plastering our backs against the wall, sucking in our guts and staring down in terror at our toes. The tires of the widest vehicle passed within six inches of our feet, and much to my dismay I could actually *feel* the breeze as all three side-view mirrors (converted suddenly into lethal weapons) fanned my solar plexus.

Farther down the hill, still inching along like a pair of Nike-shod banana slugs, we began to pass one silver store after another. Taxco is the silver jewelry capitol of the known Universe, which was why we were there in the first place. As we passed these shops, filled from floor to ceiling with bright, glittering bangles, my wife, a charter member of Shopper's Anonymous, began to glow herself with radioactive enthusiasm. Before I could stop her she had ducked inside one of the three hundred wholesale establishments and I had no choice but to follow.

When she was about to enter the fifth silver emporium, I finally felt compelled to put my foot down.

"No more silver stores till tomorrow," I said.

"But it's safer than walking the streets," she said.

"What about the sculptor?" I complained.

"He's not going anywhere," Lucy pointed out.

"That may be," I replied ill-humoredly, "but I'm all shinyed-out. I can't take it any more. The glare is killing me. I'm going snow-blind, for Christ's sake."

"Then put on your sun-glasses."

"I left them at the hotel."

"Then wait outside. And keep your elbows in," Lucy added, ducking inside the door, her face a mask of sheer stark shopping madness.

An hour later we finally managed to reach the square, without being crippled, or de-boned or bankrupted, and flagged down a passing cab.

As our taxi crawled down the scary streets I could not help but marvel aloud at the driver's extraordinary skill. Yes, the young man informed us, driving in Taxco was fraught with all manner of difficulties and dangers. Personally, he suffered from constant gastrointestinal disorders and his vehicle took its share of punishment as well. A new clutch for example lasted only six months, which was as good an excuse as any for charging us double the going rate.

After two exceedingly close calls, one with a cliff and another with a burro, we managed to arrive safely at our destination.

Vicente himself greeted us at the front door with a great display of warmth and enthusiasm. I took this to be a good sign: if he were as desperate for a sale as I believed, it would probably be possible to negotiate a good price.

Nothing could have been further from the truth.

Before business could be discussed, we were forced to take a tour of the house, especially the roof where Vicente had his workshop. Lying all over the floor of his outdoor rooftop workshop were chunks, shards and flakes of a shiny black rock which looked like congealed tar.

"*This* is *Obsidian!*" he announced dramatically. "It is extremely difficult to carve. I must use a drill with an expensive diamond bit. Even so, I often fracture a piece before I am able to complete it. Then I must start all over again. It is also a dangerous stone. Its dust is like powdered glass. I must wear a mask and protective goggles while I work on it, and even though I work outside, I must work in front of a fan in order to keep the corrosive dust from entering my lungs. Even though I wear a mask, and I am working outside."

Christ! I thought. Does this kid have a knob? How do you turn him off?

"Fascinating," I said.

Lucy gave me a meaningful look. This was not the sort of preamble which normally preceded an inexpensive purchase.

From the roof we descended down a steep narrow cement staircase to Vicente's living room. There, on a long low table he had set out seven pieces for our perusal. They were all beautiful, but only three caught my eye. One was the piece from the night before. The other two were variations on the same theme: a Jaguar Warrior embracing a jaguar and a Serpent Warrior embracing, logically enough, a snake.

"So," I said, after an appropriate interval of oohing and ahing, "how much is the eagle warrior, for example?"

Suddenly, Vicente seemed to become highly distracted. Instead of replying to my query, he began to stare down at the ground and then around the room as if he were looking for something. Patience, after many years of living in Mexico, was a virtue Lucy and I had been forced to cultivate. And so, we sat there quietly and waited for Vicente to focus on the matter at hand.

A full minute later, Vicente took a deep breath, as if with the greatest of difficulty he had finally managed to get his emotions under control, and named a figure three times higher than the one I had in mind.

"Vicente," I said pleasantly, "perhaps I should explain something."

"Yes?" he said, staring intently at the ground again.

I proceeded to explain to the idiosyncratic artist that we were not tourists, that we owned a shop in Puerto Vallarta and that we would be purchasing his work for the purposes of resale. Therefore, we were hoping to pay a wholesale price (in other words, cheap) for his work, which would enable us to sell it easily and come back in the near future to purchase more.

My little speech, I believed, which I had given on many occasions to many different artisans, had been calm, reassuring and respectful.

I must have been mistaken.

Vicente leapt to his feet and fairly exploded with outrage. "I am an artist!" he proclaimed violently. "My work is not some mass produced trinket you can find on some street corner. No one, and I mean no one, is capable of producing from this stone the depth of detail and emotion that I am!"

I refrained from mentioning that if I had not found him and his work on a street corner, I had at least found him close to one. Instead, I said in an attempt to mollify the bug-eyed artist, "Your work is exquisite. If it were not, we would not be here. We appreciate the difficulty…"

"You have no idea," he interrupted me, "of the difficulty entailed in producing such a work. Sometimes I labor on a piece for an entire week, only to see it shatter into a hundred pieces as I am applying the finishing touches. On countless occasions I, a man, have been reduced to tears by these last minute disasters. And I cannot tell you how many times my hands have been cut by the sharp edges of this difficult stone."

Vicente's over-the-top delivery had gone from violent to maudlin. Unconsciously, I began to search my pockets for a handkerchief.

"Obsidian is a cruel mistress," he went lugubriously on. "The floor of my workshop is not just covered with dust and shards. My blood…my sweat…my tears… litter the ground as well."

Christ, I'm going to throw up, I thought to myself.

"Yes, I can appreciate…" I began.

"Before I begin a new work," he interrupted me again, "I go to Santa Prisca where I get down on my knees and pray to the Virgin of Guadalupe for her guidance and her blessing. I do not exaggerate when I say that every statue of mine is imbued with a small piece of my immortal soul. For me this is not simply a means to make a living, it is part of my religion. I am a spiritual man and I take my religion very seriously."

My wife nudged me and pointed with her eyes towards the door. Apparently, she wanted to forget the whole business and get out of there before we were pierced by a chunk of bloody obsidian.

Obsidian, by the way, is the stone from which the Aztecs fashioned their knives, arrows and spears, so Lucy's fear was perhaps not so far-fetched.

I patted her knee soothingly and said to her in English, "Don't worry, honey, I don't think he's going to rip our hearts out just yet."

Vicente, meanwhile, had sat down and was staring intensely at the ground again.

"Alright, Vicente," I said, letting him know by the tone of my voice that I'd had about as much of his bullshit as I could take, and that it was time to get down to business. "What if we buy all three of these pieces? Could you possibly find it in your heart to give us a better price?"

"Ten per cent," he said glumly.

"How about twenty?"

"Fifteen."

"Okay," I said. "I'll have to give you a check."

"That's fine," he said. "You can pick up the pieces after I cash the check. How about this afternoon?"

"Sure," I said. We shook hands all around, expressed our mutual delight at having made one another's acquaintance, and beat a hasty retreat.

As we began the long climb back up to town (taxis were nowhere to be found in that neighborhood), Lucy turned to me and said, "What a weirdo!"

"Yes, he was kind of obnoxious," I agreed. "He probably watches too much television."

"I don't mean that," Lucy said. "Didn't you notice the way he kept staring at me?"

"No," I confessed. "The only thing I noticed him staring at was the floor. I thought he might be nauseous. I know he was making *me* nauseous."

"He wasn't staring at the floor," Lucy said, "he was staring at my feet."

"Are you sure?"

"Positive. It gave me the creeps. Like he was going to go for my toes or something."

"Well," I said, laughing it off, "he's definitely a character."

"Character?" Lucy said, laughing as well, "I'd say he was a bona-fide pervert."

"Well, whatever he is, he's talented. Those figures are spectacular. And so are your feet," I added diplomatically.

"And you paid a fortune for them. I hope they sell."

"Your feet? No one could put a price on those, darling."

Lucy need not have worried. All three of Vicente's pieces sold quickly, and at a premium. Two of the buyers had, in fact, been so enthralled with the gifted pervert's work, they had practically begged us to find them more. One of these avid collectors, a retired attorney from New York who looked like a cross between a Hobbit and the Pillsbury Dough Boy, actually said to me:

"I am a serious art buyer."

In our modest shop we mostly catered to clients looking for gifts. Certainly no one had ever described himself as a serious art buyer before. When Lucy asked me what exactly the over-the-hill shyster had meant, I was unable to give her an intelligent answer. So out came my trusty copy of *The Compleat Idiot's Guide to Sales and Marketing*, where I managed to find a brief definition:

Serious Art Buyer: A man or woman willing to shell out ridiculous sums of money for objects of little or no intrinsic value.

The following June once again found us in the quaint colonial city of Taxco. You would never have guessed it to see it now, but our hotel had once been the stopping place of Hollywood luminaries such as Henry Fonda and Spencer Tracy. Photographs of the handsome young stars, accompanied by glamorous-looking women (who may or may not have been their wives), were proudly displayed in the small lobby. The photos appeared to date from the early Fifties, as I'm afraid did the hotel's most recent refurbishing. But the place was clean, ideally located and charming in its own rustic, dilapidated way. The only serious drawback, as I have said, was the manger, Sr. Brussell.

This man, who insisted on speaking to us in his grotesquely butchered Spanish, labored under the mistaken impression that my wife and I were vacationing travel agents. I was, I am ashamed to admit, at least partly responsible for Sr. Brussell's confusion. Apparently, I had, in a moment of weakness, more or less implied to the man that we were, in fact, in the travel industry. "We own the largest travel agency on the Pacific Coast of Mexico," I think had been my exact words. Naturally, I had let slip this minor fib in order to obtain a discounted room-rate, which I did, and now I was paying the price.

Both Lucy and I had been anxiously looking forward to our arrival in Taxco, she for her annual silver jewelry binge, and I for my next purchase of Vicente's awesome sculptures. The morning we were preparing to see the eccentric artist, as we sat drinking coffee and admiring the superb view from our sagging terrace, I glanced down at my wife's sandal-clad feet and remarked casually, "Honey, don't you think it's time you treated yourself to a pedicure?"

"*You* want me to get a pedicure?" Lucy said with surprise; she often teased me, facetiously of course, about how cheap I was.

"Sure," I said. "Why not? You deserve it, don't you?"

"Alright," she said, " but I'd rather wait till this afternoon."

"Why wait," I said.

"Aren't we in a big hurry to go see Vicente?" she asked.

"Vicente can wait," I said gallantly. "My wife always comes first."

"Oh, I get it," Lucy said, kicking me gently in the shins. "You want me to look my best for that crazy foot-fetishist."

"Not at all," I lied. "And let's be extra careful going down those stairs today," I added. "We don't want to be bruising our toes."

"Right," Lucy said, "a bruised toe could cost you plenty."

"Please, give me a break," I said. "I just want you to look your best."

"I don't know who's sicker," Lucy said, "you or Vicente." But in the end she good-naturedly agreed to have her pedicure before we saw the sculptor.

I could see at once that the pedicure had been a terrific idea. Lucy's ruby-red toenails, peeking enticingly out from a daring pair of open-toed sandals, acted like so many little magnets, pulling Vicente's head down in a forty-five degree vertical plunge, like a monk who has suddenly been ordered by a higher power to immerse himself in prayer. Then, as he led us to the living room and offered us a seat around a new glass-topped coffee table, the distracted sculptor kept bumping into things, so intently was his gaze locked upon Lucy's freshly lacquered toes.

While I sleep-walked my way through the obligatory small talk, I could not help but wonder if Vicente had purchased the glass-top table expressly for our visit; it certainly offered a marvelous view of Lucy's feet, and it did not go at all with the rest of the décor.

"So, Vicente," I said, stroking the weird young man shamelessly, "what wonderful treasures do you have for us today?"

Vicente, business never far from his mind (no matter how entrancing the view beneath the glass-topped table), shot from his chair like a rocket and sped from the room.

While he was gone, his wife came in, introduced herself and offered us a refresco. As she stood there chatting with my wife, I found myself stealing quick furtive glances at her feet. Surprisingly, she was wearing tennis shoes and thick white socks. Either Vicente was a closet prude or else his wife was playing hard to get.

When she had gone to fetch us our cokes, I said to Lucy in English, "Listen. I've got an idea. When it's time to negotiate the price, I'm going to pretend I have to go to the bathroom, so you can…"

"No!"

"So you can ask him for a better deal."

"No!"

"Come on, what's the harm, honey. He's not going to attack you with me and his wife in the house. Maybe you can kind of, you know, rub your feet together, like you've got an itch or something."

"Are you crazy?" Lucy asked me.

Before I could reply Vicente returned carrying a cardboard box with five small statues wrapped carefully inside. As he placed them one by one atop the coffee table, I could not help but be impressed all over again by the extraordinary beauty of his work.

"Are these all you have?" I asked.

"For the moment, yes," he replied. "I've been very busy. God has been good to me. There has never been so much demand for my work."

Here we go, I thought, he's getting ready to jack up the price.

"Well, I'm interested in them all," I said. "Let's discuss price. Since we're return clients and we're talking about five pieces…"

I left the sentence unfinished, afraid that any overt reference to a reduction in price might trigger another of his psychotic episodes.

"Unfortunately," he began, "I will not be able to…"

"Excuse me, Vicente," I interrupted him, "may I use your bathroom, please?"

"Certainly," he said eagerly, "it's just down that hall to your left."

"Thank you," I said, avoiding my wife's murderous glance as I left the room.

When I returned five minutes later, I found Lucy exactly where I had left her. But Vicente was now standing in the center of the room, his posture unnaturally erect as if were in the middle of delivering a sermon.

" I was just explaining to your wife," he said, eyeing me warily, "since your last visit the demand for my work has increased considerably and so has the price." As he named a figure, which was just over double what I had paid the previous year, I felt a sudden stab of pain in my chest, like the onset of a heart attack.

"However," he went on in his formal way, "since I regard you as very special clients, I have decided to raise the price only fifty per cent. But please," he added urgently, "do not tell anyone."

I looked from Vicente to my wife and back to Vicente again and decided that further discussion would probably prove to be counter-productive. And so, I bit the bullet, agreed to his price and brought the transaction to a quick conclusion.

Having learned from our arduous experience the year before, we had instructed the taxi to wait for us, and we were soon winding our way back up to the hotel, gently caressing cliffs, soft-shoulders and pedestrians along the way.

"So?" I asked Lucy, when my curiosity had finally gotten the better of my fear.

My wife, contrary to expectations, was no longer angry. She was, instead, bemused and a tad bewildered. Rather than taking what had occurred personally, she regarded the whole business with the dazed detachment of a naturalist who, on a stroll through the woods, has come upon, say, a woodchuck with three ears. "First," Lucy said after a long pause, "he told me flat out that I had the most beautiful feet he had ever seen."

"Wow," I said, impressed.

"The look on his face," she went on, "was...ecstatic. Like he was seeing God, or something."

"He wasn't far off there," I said, kissing her tenderly on the cheek.

"And his voice was all hoarse, as if he'd suddenly come down with bronchitis."

"Unbelievable!"

"No, wait," Lucy said. "That was nothing. What happened next was unbelievable. He's staring at my feet, practically drooling, and he says, 'I have to sculpt them!'"

"Oh my God."

"He wants me to pose for him…naked…from the shins down."

"Out of the question," I said.

"He asked if you would mind."

"Mind? Damn right I mind. I mind so much," I said with husbandly outrage, "it's going to cost that little pervert his shirt."

"What?"

"Nothing," I said quickly. "So what did you say?"

"I told him I'd have to discuss it with you, but I didn't think it was a really good idea. I was so embarrassed."

"Then what did he say?"

"Then he said…" Lucy burst out laughing. "Then he said, if I couldn't pose for him, would I consider letting him make a plaster cast of my left foot."

Perfect, I thought to myself, now I've got that greedy little bastard exactly where I want him.

"Outrageous!" I told my wife. "The nerve of that despicable dwarf. I've got a good mind to go back there and…and…"

"And ask for a bigger discount?"

The problem with Lucy was that she knew me too well.

Back at the hotel we deposited our newest acquisitions in the room and attempted to dodge, unsuccessfully, Sr. Brussell, who had been stalking me relentlessly ever since our arrival.

"You go ahead with Sr. Brussell," Lucy said, with a cruel smile on her face. "I've got a terrible head-ache."

If my wife really did have a headache, it didn't last long. The minute we had turned our backs she was off down the back stairs again, to go on a massive silver-buying binge.

Trapped like a rat in the hotel's kitchen, I had no choice but to allow the overweight and fart-plagued manager to bully me into taking an exhaustive tour of the entire establishment.

The tour began in Sr. Brussell's office, where I was loaded down like a burro with several kilos of brochures, business cards and hotel stationary. The logical time to give me all of this printed refuse would have been the end of the tour, not the beginning. As it was, for the next thirty minutes I had no choice but to lug this pile of garbage up and down flight after flight of stairs, into junior suites, out of untold master-baths, and finally inside the highlight of the entire extravaganza, the boiler room.

The boiler room was currently under repair, which explained the temporary absence of hot water. This dark, musty, windowless chamber looked like the inside of a cave and the ancient boiler like some medieval device designed to torture unrepentant heretics. Two shirtless workers covered from head to toe in black grime, though busily at work with wrenches and hammers, bore the defeated look of players going through the motions at the end of a game which has been lost in the first quarter. Sr. Brussell, responding, I imagine, to my look of dismay, proceeded to give his workers several pieces of advice in such horribly contorted Spanish that I was certain the men could have no idea what he was talking about. Then he turned to me and said something which sounded like, "This bathroom will be like a soft-boiled egg as soon as these two tongue-twisters screw a potato."

The two workers and I exchanged incredulous glances. Sr. Brussell farted loudly one time. And the tour was over.

Our only unfinished business in Taxco was to find out, for my peace of mind if nothing else, if Vicente had truly given us a discount off of his obscenely inflated prices. By chance, the waiter at our favorite *comida corrida* restaurant had a brother-in-law who did business on a regular basis with our sexually skewed sculptor. After making a series of phone calls the heavily-tipped waiter was able to confirm that we had indeed been blessed with a hefty discount, which meant that my wife's feet were now worth, bone for bone, their weight in gold.

Back home once again in Vallarta, business was brisk. I was able to unload two of Vicente's sculptures before my "serious art-buyer" from New York had even put in an appearance.

Irving—the retired attorney and I were now on a first name basis—came to the shop directly from the airport.

"I haven't even checked into the hotel yet," he told me, "I was so anxious to see the sculptures."

My client, in an attempt to give himself a *hip* appearance, had grown a short goatee. He had also tied back the six hairs, which still grew on the back of his head, into a long anemic ponytail. All and all, Irving now looked like a cross between a teapot and a Ukrainian hippie who almost survived Chernobyl.

"You're looking good, Irving," I told him.

"Thanks," he said nervously. "Did you get the sculptures?"

Irving may have been a terrific attorney in his day, but he was one of the worst negotiators I had ever known.

"Irving, I have good news and I have bad news," I announced somberly.

The ex-attorney's face turned alarmingly pale. I've gone too far, I thought; the poor man is about to have a stroke. I was no cardiologist but I seemed to remember that a stroke could impair a person's motor functions, making it difficult to perform even simple tasks—like signing a credit card voucher.

"What? What?" he demanded breathlessly.

"The good news," I said reassuringly, "is that I was able to procure three exquisite pieces. I have them hidden in the back room, away from prying eyes."

"Wonderful, wonderful," he said, sighing with relief. "What's the bad news?"

"Irving, I'm afraid that Vicente is gaining something of an international reputation. So…"

"His price has gone up," Irving interrupted me helpfully.

"Precisely. Doubled in fact," I said, speaking, in my own way, the perfect truth.

"It's to be expected," Irving said philosophically. "Let's take a look."

After Irving had left the shop three serious works of art richer, I sat down at my desk and did some arithmetic. Our profits on Vicente's five sculptures were roughly equal to what we would normally net over the course of two good months. Even though the season was just getting underway, it would almost surely be worth our while to close the shop for a few days and take a quick drive to Taxco. Before I knew it, the phone was in my hand and I was calling Vicente's neighbor—the stunted pervert was too cheap to have a phone of his own.

Contacting Vicente by phone was more easily said than done. On my first attempt, I succeeded only in reaching the neighbor's six-year-old daughter who seemed to think I was her favorite TV cartoon character. On my second try I made contact with the neighbor's husband, who was either drunk or in a partial coma.

"You're an American?" he asked.

"Yes," I said, "but…"

"I've been to the United States," he said.

"That's very nice, but…"

"I've been to Sacramento," he drawled. "San Jose. Oakland. San Luis Obisbo. Los Angeles. San Diego…"

"That's great," I broke in, "your neighbor, Vicente, is the…"

"Modesto. San Antonio. Dallas. Houston…"

I hung up the phone while he was still in Texas.

An hour later I tried again. This time the neighbor herself got on the line. After making me spell my name six times, she finally agreed to fetch Vicente.

"*Amigo*," I said expansively, "*Como le va?*"

"I'm unbelievably busy," the unctuous worm informed me rudely. "The demand for my work has sky-rocketed. Everyday I thank God for the tremendous talent He has given me."

"How wonderful," I said. "I'm so happy for you."

"One day they will be displaying my statues in museums throughout Latin America."

"Well," I said, gritting my teeth, "I just couldn't be more pleased, Vicente."

"I am very busy right now." The sculptor's rudeness knew no bounds. "What is it you wanted to talk to me about?"

"Well," I began casually, "I was wondering if you remembered the last conversation you had with my wife?"

"Yes?" he said uncertainly.

"The reason I'm calling, Vicente," I cooed, like the spider to the fly, "is that I have a little proposition for you."

The fourteen-hour drive from Puerto Vallarta to Taxco proved to be grueling in more ways than one. Aside from the normal inconveniences (malodorous pig trucks, creeping gas tankers, demented bus drivers), there were certain matters which my wife wished to discuss and which I wished to avoid until the last possible moment. Our verbal fencing began just outside of Tepic, continued all the way through Guadalajara and lasted almost halfway to Mexico City. Finally, just as we were passing the turnoff to Morelia, Lucy said, "Stop the car."

"But, honey," I protested, "we're making good time."

"Stop the car," she repeated.

"Alright," I said, "but let's wait till the next gas station."

After we had gassed-up and visited the rest rooms, we parked in the shade of a jacaranda tree.

"First tell me about the shoes," my wife said.

"The shoes," I said, pausing to take a deep breath. "The shoes are part of the deal."

"What deal?"

"The deal I made with Vicente."

"Tell me about it."

Vicente, I proceeded to explain, had agreed to drop everything and turn out twenty different pieces for me, all of them original and of the finest quality. In addition, he had agreed to revert back to the price we had first paid, which was less than half the going rate.

"And he agreed to do all that just for two pairs of old shoes?" my wife asked archly.

"Not exactly, honey," I said.

"Not exactly, honey?" she repeated. Lucy, I am not ashamed to say, is one of the sweetest human beings I have ever known. She can, however, when the mood strikes her, become somewhat stubborn.

"Yes, well, there were some other considerations," I said feebly.

"Such as?"

"Well, it's kind of complicated," I said, which was no exaggeration.

"I'm listening."

"Okay," I said. "You know how when a novel is made into a motion picture, the writer still retains ownership of the novel. All he's done is sold the movie rights. It's still his book; it's just not his movie."

"Uh-huh."

"Okay. So I've sold, as it were, to Vicente the…ah… how shall I put this…the *artistic* rights to your left foot."

"What?"

"It's still your foot," I rushed to explain. "I mean, he won't actually own it. He just gets to photograph it and make a, you know, a kind of plaster cast of it, from which he can make a sculpture or a bust—I'm not sure if that's the right word for the statue of a foot. I think a bust is more a head and shoulders kind of thing. But anyway, in exchange for two old pairs of shoes, the photos and the plaster cast, plus whatever use he chooses to make of that, we wind up with…"

"I don't believe this," Lucy said. Although her voice was calm I could tell she was not pleased.

"Hey, it's just a business…"

"You sold him my left foot?"

"No, no," I said, "you don't understand. He doesn't get to keep the actual foot. Like I explained, all he gets are the artistic rights."

"You're out of your goddamn mind!" Lucy said. I knew she was genuinely upset now, because she rarely if ever used that kind of language.

"You know," I said, "I gave this all a lot of thought before making the deal. And I came to the conclusion that we'd judged Vicente too harshly. I really think that the way he looks down at your feet is more a spiritual expression than a sexual one. I mean, looking down like that, there's a certain humility involved, a true religious quality. It's as if, standing there before the perfection of your feet, he enters into…a state of grace; as if he were looking upon, not just a mortal foot, but the actual face of God. It seems to me that's how St. Francis of Assisi must have felt when he looked about him at Creation, at the birds and the animals and the, you know…nature in general."

"I don't believe what I'm hearing," Lucy said furiously. "First he's 'that greedy little pervert' and now he's some kind of saint. This is the worst bullshit I've ever heard in my life. I feel like Demi Moore in that stupid movie."

"I agree," I said."

"You *agree*?"

"Yes," I said judiciously, "the premise of that movie was totally ridiculous. I mean, if I'd been Demi Moore, *I* would have paid to sleep with Robert Redford, even if he was a little past his prime. Personally, I never found her all that attractive…"

"I want a divorce."

"Honey, I think we're over-reacting a little here. After all, it's just your foot. And he can only go up as far as mid-shin. I've got *that* in writing," I added smugly.

"Only my foot? Only my foot?"

"Yes. And all he's going to do is wrap it in gauze and put some plaster over it. His hands will never actually touch skin."

"You have absolutely no respect for me, do you?"

"Of course I respect you," I said sincerely. "I mean, you know there are lines I would never cross."

"What lines?"

"Well, if he'd wanted to lick your toes, for example. I have far too much regard for you as a human being to ever barter away your dignity. Or my own, for that matter," I added self-righteously.

Lucy just sat there for several moments glaring at the windshield, so I said experimentally, "Okay, well I'm glad we got that off our chests," and started the car.

"Turn off the engine," Lucy said.

"Honey, we're losing valuable time."

"Turn off the engine."

"Come on. We don't want to be driving on that awful road in the dark."

"I'm not going to do it."

I turned off the engine.

For almost twenty minutes we sat there in total silence. Finally, I glanced over at Lucy and saw that she had tears in her eyes. It was then that I began to feel like a bona-fide louse. What had I been thinking? How could I have become so obsessed with making a profit that I would jeopardize something as precious as my marriage? What had happened to my priorities, to my values? To be a success: was it really so important? Was it more important than my wife's happiness? Was it more important than the only decent relationship I'd ever had in my life?

"God," I said, my own voice choking with unshed tears, "I'm sorry, honey. You're right. I'm so sorry. I don't know what happened to me. Somehow I just got carried away, lost my sense of proportion."

"I love you," Lucy said, throwing her arms around me.

"I love you, too," I said, starting the car. "And as for that pervert Vicente, he'll just have to settle for the shoes and photographs."

The next morning, after explaining to the Englishman that we were too short on time to inspect the imported toilet seats he had installed in all of the junior suites, we paid a short visit to the bank and then headed directly for Vicente's house.

The self-important little twit was naturally delighted to see us. After dispensing rapidly with the small talk, he brought out the twenty sculptures and arranged them neatly on top of the coffee table. Creating twenty original works all with either Aztec or Mayan motifs had been no easy task. The process, Vicente explained to us, had left him "aesthetically exhausted", whatever the hell that meant. In any case, he had done a superb job. Eagles, jaguars, serpents, armadillos, bats, warriors and priests of every description had turned an ordinary coffee table into a veritable microcosm of pre-Hispanic Mexican culture. Vicente had even, in his determination not to repeat himself, created several tableaus depicting a man and a woman. In each case the man was on his knees while the woman stood proudly before him. Not surprisingly, the men's lips had been carved in close proximity to the women's feet.

"Wonderful," I exclaimed. "Marvelous. Stupendous. Magnificent. Not even Michael Angelo," I poured it on like imitation maple syrup over a stack of hot cakes, "Could have produced such an amazing variety of aesthetically perfect pieces in such a short amount of time. Wrap them up."

Bursting at the seams with pride and burning from within with anticipation for what was to come, Vicente quickly wrapped up all twenty statues and packed them carefully in four small cartons.

Now it was my turn, and I prayed inwardly that no matter what the outcome of my desperate ploy, it would not, even in the worst of cases, terminate in violence. Doing my best to appear calm and self-assured, I reached into a large shopping bag and withdrew ten substantial stacks of one hundred peso notes, placing them side-by-side at one end of the table. Then I removed two well-worn pairs of women's shoes and placed them side-by-side at the opposite end.

Like a spectator at an especially exciting tennis match, Vicente's intense gaze shifted abruptly back and forth between the stack of bills and the old shoes. He's going to give himself a good case of whiplash, I thought as, torn between the twin towers of lust and greed, he could not decide where to rest his eyes. While he was thus engaged in abusing his cervical vertebrae, I withdrew an instamatic camera from the same bag and proceeded to take four photos of my wife's left foot from a variety of distances and angles. When the photos had developed themselves, I placed them on the table as well in a nice neat row. This was Lucy's cue, agreed upon the night before (along with a vacation to New York the following June) to get up and leave the room. We had decided that she would wait for me outside in the taxi while whatever was going to happen next did in fact happen.

"Vicente," I said, "I have something to tell you."

The demented sculptor slowly raised his head. Like a man coming out of a trance, his eyes took several moments to focus. I really believe that the sight of the money, the shoes and the photographs had been all but too much for him. Suddenly, he began to look all around, clearly bewildered.

"Where's your wife?" he asked desperately.

"That's what I have to tell you," I said gravely. "My wife, like yourself, Vicente, is a very devout Catholic. After I explained to her the nature of the arrangement we had made, she felt compelled to consult with her priest. I am afraid that the Padre was of the opinion that the plaster caste would be in serious violation of Papal Canons 1345 and 1479, the ones dealing with graven images and such. In fact, after extensive consultations with the Bishop of Tepic, he absolutely forbade my wife to even consider the procedure. I'm very sorry."

"But we had a deal," Vicente said angrily.

"Yes we did," I said somberly, "but being a good Catholic yourself, I'm sure you can understand the difficulty of my wife's position. Not to put too fine a point on it, God, I fear, has intervened. And so all I can say to you, Vicente, is this: you may take the money and the photographs and the shoes; or you may reject them. In either case I will respect your decision and bear you no ill-will; and neither, I am certain, will the Virgin of Guadalupe."

Vicente glared at me for several moments before switching his wild eyes to the objects sitting atop the coffee table. It could not have been an easy decision for him, but in the end he really hadn't much choice.

When, reluctantly, he shook my hand to finally seal the bargain, I looked him directly in the eye and said, "Vicente, I want you to know that I'm really sorry. And in order to make it up to you, the minute I get home"—I lowered my voice to a confidential whisper—"I'm going to Fed-Ex you Lucy's favorite pair of red pumps."